MW01601936

Raggin' the Blues

ᗰᗰ

Legendary Country Blues
and
Ragtime Musicians

AVISSON YOUNG ADULT SERIES

Raggin' the Blues

~~~

Legendary Country Blues
and
Ragtime Musicians

Mary Wilds

Avisson Press, Inc.
Greensboro

First edition
Printed in the United States of America
ISBN 1-888105-47-X

Library of Congress Cataloging-in-Publication Data

Wilds, Mary, 1960-
    Raggin' the blues : legendary country, blues and, ragtime musicians / Mary Wilds.
        p. cm. -- (Avisson young adult series)
    Includes bibliographical references and indexes.
    ISBN 1-888105-47-X (pbk.)
    1. Country musicians--United States--Biography--Juvenile literature. 2. Blues musicians--United States--Biography--Juvenile literature. 3. Jazz musicians--United States--Biography--Juvenile literature. [1. Musicians. 2. Country music. 3. Blues (Music) 4. Jazz.] I. Title. II. Series.

ML3929.W55 2001
781.64'092'273--dc21
[B]

                                                00-066416

Photo credits: AP/ Wide World Photos.

Contents

Big Bill Broonzy near the height of his early success. Note the sophisticated style of dress; later, when audiences wanted a country, down-home sound, Broonzy was capable of making a stage appearance in a cotton shirt and overalls.

William "Big Bill" Broonzy

When you write about me, please don't say I'm a jazz musician. Don't say I'm a musician or a guitar player—just write Big Bill was a well-known blues singer and player and has recorded 260 blues songs from 1925 up till 1952 ... he was liked by all the blues singers ... he was a happy man. —William "Big Bill" Broonzy

Black and white film footage shows "Big Bill" Broonzy playing single guitar on a porch, something he must not have done very often. Broonzy, though a country blues artist, spent most of his career as an urban musician, composing for the jukebox and playing in Chicago jazz clubs. He may not have played on a country porch since his young manhood in Arkansas but on film, the setting hardly matters. As he sings "Worried Man Blues," "How You Want It Done," and "Henry & Blues in E," the real Bill Broonzy easily shines through. Whether playing solo, backed by a combo, in a club or on his own, Broonzy was that rare performer who knew how to be likeable on and off stage. Neither fan nor foe ever had a bad word to say about him. Then again, perhaps the world was simply a mirror which shone back at Bill Broonzy what light he gave out. He told the man who helped him author a book that he'd rather have friends than money. He got his wish.

William Lee Conley Broonzy was born in 1893 (or 1898, according to the papers his sister produced after his death) in Scott, Mississippi, one of 21 children (five of whom died in infancy) and the male half of a pair of twins.

Broonzy always said his parents had met during "slave time," or while they were slaves. According to the story, the two got together when Broonzy's mother, unable to keep up with the pace of cotton-picking, had gotten a beating. The next day, Broonzy's father picked his share of cotton more quickly than usual. He then crawled through the grass to help her pick her share.

"Often I have heard my mother say, 'Any time a man takes a chance on his life to help me, he's good enough for me to marry and have a baby for,'" Broonzy wrote in his autobiography, *Big Bill Blues*. His co-author, Yannick Bruynoghe, gently disputes this story in the book's foreword. Had Broonzy's parents met while still enslaved, his mother would have been much too young "to mix love and cotton-picking," Bruynoghe said.

Mother Broonzy obviously had plenty of babies, as did her husband. Father Broonzy fathered six additional children outside their marriage. "My mother found that out [about his father's second family] after he died," Broonzy wrote.

"If she had known about [the other children beforehand]," he added wryly, "he might have died earlier." (One of Broonzy's half-brothers was the blues musician Washboard Sam, with whom Broonzy played and recorded while living in Chicago.)

Broonzy's family moved to Arkansas, where he grew up in farm country. By all accounts Bill's childhood was happy, though hardly carefree. He was working by the age of seven, for a white neighbor. By the age of 10, he and a friend were making their own instruments. He made a fiddle out of a cigar box for himself and a guitar out of "good" boxes for his buddy, Louis Carter.

"We would play for the white people's picnics and sometime they would have two [performance] stages," he wrote. "Negroes would be on one side and whites on the other."

The boys played for food and for hand-me-down clothes, but one day all that would change. A sympathetic and generous white fan came to one of their performances and presented them with a real guitar and fiddle. The boys kept to their homemade instruments for a while because they had no idea how to play the real thing. It would take them three months to get the hang of playing the new instruments.

Broonzy's mother had never approved of his playing; because of her devout Christian beliefs, she thoughts blues to be the 'devil's music'. She wished desperately that he'd give up performing. By 1915, she got her wish. Broonzy married, started a family, and acquired a share-cropping arrangement with a local farmer. He also resolved to be a preacher and forego "sinful" activities, like music. His retirement, though, was short-lived:

one day, a local man offered him fifty dollars and a new fiddle if he would perform at a four-day picnic. His wife, Ruth, called Guitrue in one biography, accepted the offer for him, took the money and spent it. Broonzy was obliged to play so that the debt could be paid. The experience apparently jump-started his desire to make music. Broonzy's mother still disapproved, however, so strongly that whenever he came to visit her he'd leave his guitar outside the house.

Broonzy's share-cropping days were numbered. After drought ruined the harvest, Broonzy did a stint in the Arkansas coal mines. In 1917, he enlisted in the army. When he mustered out two years later, he found he could not bear the thought of returning to the South. Broonzy, being African-American, had had his share of bad times there. He once recounted the time he'd found himself in north Arkansas, in a town where blacks were not welcome. Anxious to buy a meal, he walked from establishment to establishment, only to find that none of them would serve him. Finally, at the train yard, he met up with a man who frankly told him he was in danger and had better hide. The man shut up Broonzy in a large box and warned him not to leave until he was told to. The man then told the mob that came looking for Broonzy that the "Negro" they were seeking had gone in the opposite direction. He gave Broonzy food and water and kept him hidden for two days, until he was finally able to sneak him into a box car. The man gave him food to tide him over, $5, and a warning never to come back, which Broonzy heeded. This nameless man also told Broonzy that he himself had been raised to hate blacks, but figured that Broonzy was one black man who badly needed a friend. Broonzy always used the story as an example of how friends, not money, make you rich.

Broonzy was anxious to go north, so, in 1920, he moved to Chicago and took a day job with the Pullman Rail Company. After some practice and mentoring he snagged an audition with Mayo Williams at Paramount Records. This experience was hardly a success. Williams bluntly told him he wasn't any good and to find something else to do. But Broonzy persisted, and after a time convinced Williams to give him a second audition. This time he brought along a friend, John Thomas, but the two failed the audition together.

In 1922, Williams finally agreed to record them. Their two releases, "House Rent Stomp" and "Big Bill Blues" earned Broonzy no money but did move off the shelves: Broonzy made sure of it by buying "every [record] I found that was for sale," he said. Broonzy's pal Thomas wheedled $100 out of Williams by telling him he needed money to bury his father. (Thomas' father had died when Thomas was 12.) In 1926, Broonzy made a new record and earned a $15 royalty this time around. In the late 1920s, he recorded four more songs.

Blues historian Sam Charters would later write that Broonzy's first recordings "were the most unpromising first records ever made by a blues singer."

"He was terrible," Charters wrote in his 1959 book, *The Country Blues*. "Arkansas has never had much of a blues tradition so Bill had to learn to sing by listening to records. He was trying to imitate Blind Lemon [Jefferson] but he didn't have Lemon's voice."

By 1930 Broonzy was working for a grocer and still looking for a record deal. Lester Rose, a partner in the Melrose Music Publishing Company and recording director for Chennet and Champion Records, let him record four songs. The records sold poorly but Rose stuck with Broonzy, recording him again two years later. That same year Broonzy recorded with the American Record Company (ARC) in New York and at last began to make headway. He would record frequently during the late 1930s, having established his own style: "Big Bill" had become a warm, ingratiating blues singer, Charters wrote.

Broonzy's career took off at a time when the record industry was in trouble. Blues records sold poorly during the Depression, and new releases slowed to a trickle. The six Bill Broonzy songs released by ARC in the early '30s, including "Bull Cows" and "Mistreatin' Mama Blues," sold well enough to earn their maker royalties. Broonzy now had a piano player, Black Bob, in his group, so his music was more polished. Having adopted a more urban sound, he was using larger groups on his records, including four- or five-piece jazz and swing groups. He began to write songs for his half-brother, Washboard Sam, and two friends, Jazz Gillum and Tampa Red.

Sam (real name Robert Brown) showed up in Chicago in 1932 while Bill was still working in the mills. He was just twenty-two and playing the washboard around town. Bill wrote songs for him, played guitar on most of his records and appeared with him live. Sam signed on with Bluebird Records and had a few hits: "Back Door," "Just Got to Hold You" and "Mecca Flats Blues." Sam quit the business in 1947, joined the Chicago police force and moved with his family to the city's southside.

Sam's half-brother was successful enough that rival record companies were trying to duplicate his sound with their own singers, Peetie Wheatstraw in particular. Charters wrote that during his busiest periods Broonzy copyrighted about 300 songs. He became a fixture at Chicago jazz clubs like the Blue Note, and counted jazz greats Benny Goodman and Count Basie among his fans. Duke Ellington is said to have dropped in on one of Bill's sets one night and said, "Oh, that Bill. There's only one of him. I love him."

Tall, dark-skinned and broad-shouldered, Broonzy was a noticeable man in Chicago. He was known — and loved — for helping musicians new to Chicago find their way. Musician J.B. Lenoir was working at a Chicago meat-packing plant when he met Bill Broonzy. "Bill played on Lake Street [then]," he'd say. "Big Bill take me [under his wing] and I played [with him] as long as I wanted to play." Singer Memphis Minnie (Minnie McCoy) was a particular favorite of Bill's. "Memphis Minnie can pick a guitar and sing as good as any man I've ever heard," Broonzy said of her. "She can make a guitar cry, moan, talk and whistle the blues."

He and Minnie engaged in a sort of "battle of the blues" in 1933, on June 26, Bill's birthday. Onlookers worried that a contest between a man and a woman was not fair, but on that day the woman won.

"The hall was crowded, everything was free and all the musicians could get in the place was there," Broonzy remembered. "[Two friends] went to the stand, picked Minnie up and carried her around the hall until her [jealous] husband said, 'She can walk.'" Broonzy and Minnie became friends and went on to play clubs together around the country.

Broonzy played back-up guitar for another Chicago singer, Lil Green, for about two years. He wrote songs for her — "My Mellow Man" and "Give Your Mama One More Smile," and arranged others. Later, when Lil had gone on to New York and a bigger band, Broonzy went to see her at the Apollo Theater in Harlem. "She was glad to see old Bill," he remembered, "and it made me feel good to know that she hadn't forgotten the ones she'd started out with."

Not all of Broonzy's good deeds went unpunished. Blues musician Tommy McClennon, up from Mississippi, accompanied Broonzy to a party. Despite Broonzy's pleas that he changed the lyrics, McClennon sang a controversial song that so inflamed the crowd they broke McClennon's guitar.

Broonzy's music had not made him rich — he worked as a molder, cook, piano mover and porter among other things — but it did get him noticed. In 1939, he was invited to appear in a "Spirituals to Swing" concert at the famous Carnegie Hall. The concert was billed as a celebration of rural blues and jazz. Its performers were introduced accordingly. "Big Bill" Broonzy, top-selling artist for Vocalion Records and a favorite on jukeboxes around the country, was presented to the crowd as an ex-sharecropper. Broonzy handled the situation with his usual aplomb. Later, when two young fans cornered him and asked him to sing some sharecropper songs, he said he didn't dare — he might be sent back to the farm. (The main attraction of that evening night was Huddie Ledbetter, better known as Leadbelly. He'd been brought up from the Louisiana State Penitentiary for the occasion by men who recorded songs for the Library of Congress.)

The same year as his Carnegie Hall appearance Broonzy performed in a film, "Swingin' the Dream." He played in Arkansas in 1940, where a guest-of-honor was his mother. "She just stood there at the door, she didn't come in, she just stood there," he said. "When they found out who she was they didn't charge her nothin'." It is unknown whether Mother Broonzy came around to Bill's point of view about blues music, but Broonzy must have appreciated her being there.

By the late 1940s, Broonzy's music had fallen out of fashion. Having booked a visit to Iowa State College in Ames, accompanying an "I Come to Sing" group out of Chicago, he decided he liked the campus well enough to stay on for a while — as a janitor. His friends were horrified, but Broonzy, a frequent guest of the college's president and a semi-celebrity on campus, saw it as his chance to finally "go to college." During his youth he'd worked for a white family which, to his everlasting envy, sent its children to medical school, law school and teachers' college.

Besides, he wouldn't stay there for long. He was writing new tunes because a folk revival was underway. Broonzy, ever the canny performer, restyled himself as a folk singer. He even changed his style so he'd sound more like Josh White, a popular black singer of the day who mixed blues and folk. And if he had to portray himself as a sharecropper to sell records, so be it. (He told a British writer that he'd been a farmer until 1946.)

The strategy worked: Broonzy became one of the more successful personalities of the folk movement.

Broonzy recorded dozens of new songs, toured Europe, played in Paris and visited Africa, which he loved. He was interviewed about the universal appeal of blues — "A cry's a cry in any language," he said. He got glowing critical notices.

"[Broonzy's] voice possessed all the strength and virility needed for the toughest blues," Max Jones wrote in *Melody Maker* after a 1958 concert. "Bill displayed flexibility, inventiveness and an expressive range far beyond what was expected."

Broonzy grew so popular in Europe that when British actor John Neville appeared on a Chicago talk show, he quite confidently said, "Everyone knows Big Bill. Who doesn't?"

"Ninety-nine out of a hundred of his countrymen have never heard of him," the show's host, writer Studs Terkel, told his flabbergasted guest. (It's a situation that goes on today; a Rhode Island blues singer went to Finland for a concert appearance only to find he was a star in that country.)

Broonzy even wrote a book, with the help of a European: Yannick Bruynoghe, editor of a Belgian jazz magazine. Bruynoghe met Broonzy when he came to Brussels, befriended him and encouraged him to write letters. The book that ensued from their correspondence, *Big Bill Blues, William Broonzy's Story*, was published in England in 1955.

"I was thrilled by his wonderful personality," Bruynoghe said. "I persuaded him to write [letters]. He was quite enthusiastic about it ... I'm glad to insist on the fact that there has been no tape recorder used . . . Bill was writing himself [sic] most of the things."

But the good times were ending by July, 1958. Broonzy was quite ill. His British friends, fearing for his financial well-being, organized a benefit concert for him.

"Please don't think hard of me for not writing you all," he wrote when he learned of their efforts. "I can't see, I am almost blind, and my mind is not so good. I am so nervous."

Broonzy died of lung cancer on Aug. 14, 1958. His services were held at the big chapel in Chicago's Metropolitan Funeral Parlor. Muddy Waters and Tampa Red were pallbearers. One of the highlights of the service was gospel great Mahalia Jackson's version of "Just a Closer Walk with Thee."

Bill Broonzy lived in an era when men of his station and color had a difficult, if not impossible, time getting ahead. Broonzy dealt with the many obstacles in his life with a good humor rare in any man. The story is told of his meeting Studs Terkel (who later wrote a tribute to his friend Bill) on a Chicago street corner. An Illinois state senator who happened to be passing by greeted Terkel and said, gesturing to Broonzy, "So this is your boy, eh?"

Before Terkel could stammer out a response, Broonzy took over. "That's right," he said, not a bit non-plussed. "He may not look it but he's my father." The befuddled senator tossed out one more pleasantry before walking away.

Elizabeth Cotten, shown here in her nineties, still was able to sing and play her signature song, "Freight Train".

Elizabeth "Libba" Cotten

Nobody did teach me. Everything I know, I learned all by myself, so I give myself the credit.
—Elizabeth Cotten.

From an early age, Elizabeth Cotten knew how to play the cards that life dealt her. She wanted to learn to play the banjo, but the only instrument available was a homemade one. Because she was left-handed there was no one to teach her how. Even worse, the banjo in question belonged to her older brother, who was right-handed. Left-handed people need to reverse the order of the strings in any instrument they play. Cotten's brother refused to let her do so. Elizabeth solved the problem by turning his banjo upside down and puzzling out a way she could play it.

"I lay [the banjo flat] on my lap," she told Laura Weber during a 1969 broadcast of *Guitar, Guitar*. After devising a fingering method that would work for her, Elizabeth turned the banjo upright again, though still playing it upside down. Her style of playing, known as "Cotten picking" would not become popular until forty years after Cotten developed it as a teenager.

There is a story that Elizabeth Neville Cotten actually had no first name for the first few years of her life. Her parents, unable to agree on a name for her, called her "Little Sis," "Babe" and "Shug." This lasted until Elizabeth entered school.

She came home one day and announced that from now on she'd be Elizabeth.

The town in which she lived, Chapel Hill, North Carolina, had no television, no radios and little entertainment beyond what each individual provided for him or herself. Almost everyone Cotten knew was a musician. The men on her mother's side of the family played banjos and fiddles. "My [brothers and sisters] all played," she would tell Weber. "And each one played different."

Depending on who is telling her story, Elizabeth was born either in 1891, 1893 or 1895, which would put her in her early, mid or late 90s when she finally received a Grammy for one of her records. No matter what the true date of her birth might have been, the North Carolina of her youth must have been a far cry from what it is today.

Cotten told Weber that most city blocks had one house on them and that everyone knew each other, blacks and whites. Elizabeth attended school as long as she could, through the fourth grade. She then quit to go to work, probably as a domestic. The money she earned from her first job was enough to buy a guitar.

"I'd sit up late at night," she explained during a 1980 interview. "Music is a funny thing. It's something you love ... comes from inside of you. And you can shut your eyes, and go with it, and repeat it. I'd pretend I was pickin' up my guitar and keep right up with the tune.

Thanks to the guitar, Cotten's mother "didn't

get no rest. She'd say, 'put that thing down and go to bed, babe.'"

Cotten was probably most influenced by traveling musicians, medicine shows, minstrel shows, local pickers and her family. She wrote a song herself, "Freight Train," when she was only 12 years old. "Where I lived the freight train would keep me awake at night," she explained.

Cotten married Frank Cotten when she was 15. She gave birth to her only child, Lilly (or Lillie) a year later. It was about this time that she stopped playing her music. A deacon in her church (Cotten was a Baptist) had given her dire warnings about the fate of her soul: she could not continue with music and expect to go to heaven. Burdened by the demands of family and piety, Cotten put her guitar aside. For years she never sang outside of church.

If she was ever bitter over her decision, Cotten never said. Nor did she speak often of the tribulations that followed. Her marriage to Frank Cotten ended and Libba became a single mother. There were few options open to black women of her era, but Cotten took advantage of what she could. She worked as a servant and nursemaid to white families, mostly in North Carolina.

Eluzabeth moved to Washington, D.C. at some point, and got a job in a department store there. One day, a Washington matron and her two children came into the store to buy dolls. The younger child, a girl, wandered away while the dolls were being wrapped and Cotten located her quickly and efficiently. The matron expressed her gratitude with a job offer which Cotten accepted.

By pure chance, the matron was Ruth Crawford Seeger, considered by peers to be the most significant female composer of the 20th century. The children were Penny and Peggy Seeger, half-siblings of Pete Seeger, who would win fame with his political activism and as the writer of such songs as "We Shall Overcome" and "Where have all the Flowers Gone?" Peggy and her older brother, Mike, were future folk musicians themselves.

Ruth Crawford Seeger, the first woman to win a Guggenheim fellowship for music composition, had been hiring housekeepers more or less full-time since her marriage to Charles Seeger, a musicologist and father of Pete, and the births of her three children. A modern woman in a pre-modern era, Seeger mixed work (she collaborated on folk song arrangements with the poet Carl Sandburg and folk song collectors John and Alan Lomax, and pioneered the use of American folk songs in children's music education) and family; and she needed help to do so.

Housemaids would come and go in the Seeger household, but Cotten stayed and in some respects helped the Seegers make history. Her life and fortunes became irrevocably entwined with theirs. Folk songs were part of Ruth's life's work and in Cotten she found a ready research subject. In 1950, about two years after she began working for the Seegers, Cotten was captured in a homemade tape. On it, she is exhorted by a family member to "get out the banjo and remember some of those things again."

"Oh, Libba," Ruth is heard saying (either Penny or Peggy Seeger had given her the nickname). "Sing me — just before you go — the one you were doing out in the kitchen ... and I said, now we have to get it." Cotten obligingly sings "Snake Bake a Hoecake" and "Old Cow Died," both of which Ruth used in her book *Animal Folk Songs*.

"Yes, ma'am, we used to have fun, didn't we have fun," a tired Cotten says to Ruth, probably caring less about research at that point than going home to her daughter.

Cotten had reconnected with her music by this point, something that in the Seeger household would have been awfully hard to avoid. Peggy Seeger was playing guitar at the age of ten and eventually became accomplished on banjo, Appalachian dulcimer, autoharp and concertina. Her older brother Mike was playing the autoharp at age 12. Cotten is said to have performed formally for the Seegers during a Thanksgiving get-together, probably in the 1950s. There is no apparent record of how she resolved the conflict between music and faith her pastor had given her long before. But given that Cotten was still devout, she must have found a way to resolve it all in her own mind.

Probably without intending to, she had assumed an important role in the Seeger household. It was to Cotten that a Library of Congress official turned when, despairing of Crawford Seeger's lack of interest in her appearance, the composer needed to be prepped for a meeting with important visitors. Could Cotten take Ruth in hand and persuade her to "fix up?" There's no record of Cotten's success in that matter though Ruth, whose main fashion statement was putting her hair up in braids, probably made only half-hearted attempts, even at Libba's urging.

By the early 50s Cotten's role in the family was much more serious. Ruth Seeger lost her battle with cancer in 1953. Charles Seeger kept himself going long enough to proof his wife's latest book, *Let's Build a Railroad*. Then he shut himself up in his room for several days. Only Cotten was left to run the household, which she did magnificently, as Peggy Seeger, 18 years old at the time of her mother's death, remembered.

"It was a tribute to her friendship with my mother that Libba would put up with the depression the household sank into," Peggy said. When it came to their father, though, the Seeger children were on their own, The youngest, Penny, only 10 at the time, apparently thought her mother was alive and in the hospital days after Ruth's death. A year after she died, Charles sold the house and the family scattered. Libba and the children never lived under the same roof again, which must have been hard; there was a genuine affection between them.

Mike Seeger, by now 21 years old and on his

own, had already embarked on his musical career — a career that in part included Libba, perhaps as a "thank you" for all she'd done for his family. After playing square dances in the Washington, D.C. area with his sister, Peggy, Mike formed the New Lost City Ramblers. By the late 1950s he was recording other singers, including Elizabeth. He produced her first album, "Freight Train and Other North Carolina Folk Songs and Tunes" in 1957. Cotten performed with Mike at Swarthmore College in 1960 and played clubs and festivals with the New Lost City Ramblers.

Meanwhile, Cotten's first song, "Freight Train," had become famous. Peggy Seeger had begun a career that had taken her overseas. (Her half-brother Pete's political troubles trailed behind her; U.S. custom officials once tried to take her passport. She eventually became a British citizen). She went to England in 1956 to take part in a television movie and while there joined up with a musical group that included Ewan MaColl, Alan Lomax and Shirley Collins. On tour in England, Peggy played Libba's song to enthusiastic acclaim.

One day, two young men who claimed to be fans persuaded her to sing "Freight Train" into a tape recorder. The "fans" took the song back to the United States and presented it as their own. "Freight Train" became a hit for both Rusty Draper and Chet Atkins. It was played often enough on the airwaves that Pete Seeger himself chanced to hear one of the versions. As fond of

Libba as everyone else in his family, Pete contacted lawyers and a publisher. (Seeger respected blues singers in general. One of them, Leadbelly, introduced him to the 12-string guitar.) Seeger and Libba settled for a one-third song-writing credit at the end of that particular battle. Cotten got full credit, though, when "Freight Train" appeared on a Peter, Paul & Mary album.

Cotten's fans and supporters found that her decades of inactivity had actually worked in her favor. Her style was virtually unchanged from when she was a child; this made her an important historical resource as well as an entertainer. Critics today consider her part of the Piedmont guitar movement, an early 20th century style which influenced black musicians in the Carolinas and as far west as Kentucky. Cotten continued to influence her fellow musicians in the '60s. "Her Cotten-picking style was a fairly distinctive style that caught on during the folk revival," one admirer put it.

Cotten also won audiences over with her warm stage presence. By now she had left the New Lost City Ramblers and was a solo performer. In 1963, she was on the bill at the first-ever Philadelphia Folk Festival. In 1967, when she was in her mid-70s, she recorded "Elizabeth Cotten, Volume 2: Shake Sugaree." This album was followed by another, "Volume 3: When I'm Gone." Cotten also composed songs while in her 70s; "Wilson Rag" and "Ontario Blues" were two of them.

She continued to tour in her 80s and received

even greater recognition, due largely to the efforts of her agent John Ullman, a specialist in traditional music and storytelling. When her hands gave in to age, Cotten took on an accompanist, guitarist Dana Klipp, who was already arranging and composing with Cotten's granddaughter, the traditional folk artist Johnine Rankin.

Klipp had plenty of memories and opinions of Cotten and her music. "Elizabeth was a true, original [blues] source, going back to the turn of the century," Klipp said. "Being one of the discoveries during the folk boom of the 1950s, she was able to leave behind a great recorded documentation of her playing style."

Cotten's music, he added, was "often labeled as blues, but had more ragtime influence ... Her style of playing left-handed on a right-handed guitar was unique, producing a sound unlike anything a right-handed player could simulate. This technique gives her music a softer, almost classical sound. A combination of her unparalelled technique and her custom of using light strings contributed to her sound." Cotten also gave Klipp some of the best advice on performing he ever received."'If you're up there playing, don't ever stop. Even if you make a mistake, keep on goin', cause no one will ever know.'"

When she reached her 90s, Cotten moved to Syracuse, N.Y. to be with Lillie. The city welcomed her royally, creating a special park called Libba's Grove. It was planted with ash trees. They opened the Elizabeth Cotten

Conference Opportunity Center and gave her a new Martin guitar, courtesy of the local Chamber of Commerce. She recorded "Elizabeth Cotten Live" in 1984, and a year later accepted a Grammy for the best Ethnic or Traditional Folk Recording. She played her last concert at the Philadelphia Folk Festival in 1986. The following year, her friends arranged a tribute concert for her at City College in Harlem. She died that same summer, on June 29.

"[The audience] loved her, you know," Dana Klipp said. "She liked to talk to the audience, you know. What impressed me was her gift of being able to project. It wasn't just her music, it was her entire personality and her spirituality."

She was survived by Lilly, grandchildren Rankin and Larry Ellis, her great-granddaughter Brenda Fennell, and the Seeger family.

"Libba was the most balanced person I've known," Mike Seeger wrote after her death.""She had a strong sense of herself and the order of life. She was my mother, my friend and my teacher. We are so fortunate that she was here among us."

One of Libba's friends reported having a dream where she and Libba were sitting on a porch, watching a North Carolina sunset. Libba urged her to enjoy the sunset and all its beauty; after she woke up she learned Libba had died.

Laura Weber's *Guitar, Guitar* series hosted guitarists from the world of jazz, folk, blues, classical and flamenco. In the presence of Elizabeth Cotten TV host Weber appears awestruck, mentioning once that sitting with Cotten is like sitting with a part of guitar-history itself. Cotten, for her part, plays selections like "What a Friend We have in Jesus," "Ruben," "Washington Blues," and of course, "Freight Train," with aplomb, taking the TV cameras, lights and her host in stride, full of the same equanimity she'd shown in most periods of her life, good and bad.

Rev. Gary Davis

I'm going to tell you what the blues is. It's like when you fall in love with a woman and it be so long between dates before you see her. You know you have the blues.—Rev. Gary Davis, "Oh What a Beautiful City."

Gary Davis was not a talker when it came to his childhood. Very little is known about his family, his upbringing, or the one brother who survived childhood along with Davis and became, like him, a musician. Robert Tilling, Davis' friend and biographer, said the singer spoke little, if ever, about his youth. There are reports of Davis having a grown sister, although Tilling doubts she existed.

Davis was born around April 30, 1896 (the year of his birth tends to vary a bit, depending on who is giving the account), on a small farm located between Clinton and Laurens, South Carolina. He was the son of John and Evelina Davis and the eldest of eight children, six of whom apparently died in early childhood. He seems to have gone blind when he was three weeks old, after a doctor made an error in treatment.

"I'd taken sore eyes when I was three weeks old," Davis said. "They [took] me to a doctor and the doctor put some alum and sweet milk in my eyes and they caused ulcers in my eyes. This is what caused me to go blind." Davis harbored no bitterness over the incident; he considered his disability part of God's plan.

Davis grew up in Gray Court, South Carolina, at the home of his grandmother, Evelina Cheek. His sole surviving brother is said to have died in 1930. The brother's name is not recorded in Davis' biography. Tilling suggests that Davis' parents gave him to Cheek because they were not able to raise a blind child. Davis appears to have been relatively happy; he helped his grandmother out when he could, caring for the pigs and chickens. He was playing the harmonica when he was six or seven years old. "My uncle would go into town and buy himself [a harmonica] and then he'd buy me one," Davis said. "You could get a good one for 25 cents." Davis used the instrument to imitate the livestock and call them in for feeding. Around the same time, Davis began to make his own instruments, out of pie pans, wood and copper wire. That was the one part of his childhood he was more than willing to discuss.

"I got more whippin' tearing up my grandmother's pie pans," he said. "They found I was music inclined, you understand, that I had music in me. So every time my grandmother go buy a pan she buy me one because she knowed I'd tear it up first. . . I started making guitars out of pie pans. Drill holes through a piece of timber, you know, and got me some copper wire and made some strings."

He played his first banjo when he was four years old. "First thing my mother bought me a banjo. I was only four or five years old ... I thought I was doing something with that banjo ... The first time I heard guitar I thought it was a brass band coming through," he added. "I was a small kid and I asked my mother what it was and she said it was a guitar." His mother Evelina bought him his first professional guitar, a Wabash; it would be her last gift to him before she left him in his grandmother's care for good.

Davis was singing in the local Baptist Church and playing for pocket money at picnics while he was still a boy. "That's the way I made money," he said. "Playing for white people." Davis also hung out with local musicians like Will Bonds, who taught him "Candyman." The first song he ever learned was "Little Darlin' You Don't Know My Mind."

"I remember a lot of musicians," he said. "One (Craig Fowler) was a remarkable guitar player. He was the first man I took notice of." (Despite Davis' adulation, Fowler's reputation apparently never made it out of South Carolina; very little is known about him today.)

Davis joined a local string band when he was 16: one of his bandmates was the blues guitarist Willie Walker. The experience convinced Davis that he was meant to be a soloist. "After I started working with them I thought maybe I could get them somewhere," he would say later. "I found they didn't want to go nowhere. I'm always gonna play by myself because whenever I run across nothing and I don't like it there won't be nobody to get mad."

Davis was indeed interested in earning money, but as a blind man in turn-of-the-century America, his career choices were limited. He could make brooms, he could make music or he could beg in the streets. This rather bleak future was probably on his mind when he applied to the South Carolina Institution for the Education of the Deaf and Blind, in Spartanburg, when he was 18. He stayed in school long enough to learn to read braille and to possibly teach music; he was gone in six months. The reason he always gave for dropping out was that he didn't like the food.

Davis went to Greenville and met up with, and played with, Simmie Dooley, who became one of his mentors. He married for the first time in 1919, to a Greenville woman five years his senior, Mary Hendrix. The marriage ended after a few years. All he ever told friends on the subject was "she left one blind man for another."

Davis moved to Asheville, North Carolina, and became a noteworthy figure on its streets. "Along then his voice was really strong and he would sing good ... he would sit in the square and play the guitar. Mostly he'd hold the guitar right up to his head," said Aaron Washington, one of Davis' fellow street musicians. "It got to the point where everybody seemed to like him. Wouldn't hardly anybody pass without throwing some money to him."

Davis moved on to Durham in 1931. While

there he reunited with his mother, Evelina. Davis' father was not present, probably because he had been in trouble with the law since Davis was a boy, and may have been killed by police in 1906. In Durham, Davis met Blind Boy Fuller (real name Fulton, or Fuller, Allen), a street musician like Davis. Born in 1903, Fuller had been blinded in an accident when he was in his early 20s. Married with an adopted daughter, Fuller, known for his "party blues" music, must have made an interesting foil for Davis.

Fuller used to call Davis "the Daddy of the guitar players," said Willie Trice, a fellow musician. [He was] the playingest man." Davis took Fuller under his wing and taught him to play in the key of A, among other things. The two men played on the streets near the tobacco warehouses. The tobacco industry was little impacted by the Depression and its warehouses were always full, giving Fuller and Davis ready-made patrons.

"As a man he was a good-natured fellow," Davis said of Fuller. "Well thought of and everybody liked him. He do like most blind men do when they have a family or a wife, do all they can to take care of them."

Davis returned to his Baptist roots in the 1930s and mixed gospel and blues in his playing. Those who knew Davis said his music had an unusual feel to it: his vocals were straight out of church, while his fingerpicking gave spiritual songs a bluesy feel.

Davis lived in impoverished conditions in

Durham, in various tiny, rented rooms. He was nonetheless very independent and did not like anyone leading him around. He kept on playing, too. In the mid-30's it somewhat paid off.

Davis' fellow street singer, Fuller, who also teamed with harmonica-player Sonny Terry, was recruited by a scout for American Record Company (ARC) in 1935. ARC asked Davis along as a friend and to play back-up guitar for Fuller's recording session in New York City. Davis, who stayed on the corner of 133rd Street and 7th Avenue during his stint in New York, recorded 14 solo tracks and played guitar for Fuller and another musician, Bull City Red, during a three-day period.

But Davis went away furious with the financial arrangements. He had been paid a flat fee of $50, while Fuller earned royalties. He held a long-lasting emnity for the ARC scout, J.B. Long, thinking that the man had cheated him.

"I thought fifty dollars was some money," he said. "When I found out that he was getting the royalties and I wasn't getting but the fifty dollars. [Long] had me covered on that, you understand, but I waked up. He never got me no more."

Davis may have had a point; other musicians said money had a habit of disappearing when it was under Long's care. For his part, Long, who became Fuller's manager, claimed that Davis was talented but difficult to work with (he would keep playing when the recording was through and wouldn't stop unless someone told him to); that he wouldn't calm down, that he insisted on singing only spirituals, and that his records didn't have much commercial potential.

Meanwhile, Fuller went on to become one of the more recorded bluesmen of his era. Although he still liked Fuller personally, Davis would never regard his friend in the same manner again. "He done pretty good but he would have done better if I could keep him under me," Davis later sniffed. "After he learned a few things he figured that he could make it [on his own]."

Davis returned to Durham and in 1937 was playing with harmonica virtuoso Sonny Terry, whom he must have met through Fuller, their mutual friend. Davis played the harmonica all his life but never made any recordings with it. That same year he was ordained a minister, and this event cemented his determination to play gospel songs. In 1939, J.B. Long, still respectful of Davis' guitar talent, asked to record him again. Davis, hardly one to forgive and forget, said no. His friend, Fuller, died of a kidney ailment two years later.

Davis met his second wife, Annie Bell Wright, at a revival meeting in Raleigh in 1942. (Davis was spending more of his time visiting churches and preaching.) They were married a year later but had no children.

Annie Davis' homemaking skills and motherly personality served her and her husband well, particularly after they moved to New York in 1944. Annie got a job as a cook so they were able to rent an apartment at East 196th Street in the Bronx, their home for the next 20 years. "I never heard nothing good about New York before I came here," Davis said. He played regularly on the streets of Harlem and found the experience quite different than his days in North Carolina.

"I got run off the street by police and put in jail," he said. "All kinds of stuff like that. Still kept on playing, though."

It was in Harlem also "where I got most of my robbin' done," he later said. "I have had five guitars ... stolen. Every time I sat down someone took something." It was rumored by some that at this time Davis began to carry a gun, though his 1992 biography makes no mention of this. Later on Davis moved his show to midtown Manhattan, where he took a post outside a guitar store near Tin Pan Alley. More than once, if he fell asleep, someone would make off with his Gibson guitar. The owner of the store, Eddie Bell, would let him pick out a new guitar and hold it for him. Davis would come back to the store to play his guitar and customers would donate change for the purchase.

Davis was a teacher at songster Brownie McGhee's Home of the Blues, in the 1940s; McGhee was one of his former pupils, and called Davis an excellent teacher. He recorded "Civil War March" in 1945, though it would not be released on an album (Folkways Records) 'til 1967. He recorded two songs for the Lennox Label in January of 1949, a session that was probably arranged by McGhee. He played a memorial concert for Huddie "Leadbelly" Ledbetter in 1950 and impressed more than a few people with his appearance.

"A single spotlight was there for Davis, who emerged from behind the curtain," said an onlooker, John Cohen. "We sensed his blindness and were stunned by his guitar-playing. There was no explanation of who he was or how he got there."

By the early '50s Davis was part of a crowd of bluesmen and folksingers who gathered regularly at the apartment of Leadbelly's niece, Tiny Robinson. Woody Guthrie, John Lee Hooker and Brownie McGhee were among those who enjoyed stopping by.

Davis was finally in the right place at the right time. He became a major figure of the then-burgeoning folk movement, playing all the major festivals (including Newport and Philadelphia) and recording for the Vanguard, Folkways and Bluesville labels. He joined up with old friend Sonny Terry to make a record for the Stinson label. Artists like John Cephas and Dave Van Ronk studied his fingerpicking and repertoire. The Davis household became a hip place for young musicians hang out; they could enjoy Annie's hospitality and Gary's guitar skills. One of Davis' disciples was a very young Janis Ian, who scored pop hits with "Seventeen" and "Society's Child."

Davis was playing less often on the streets but his presence there had gotten some notice. "I've often heard people say it's a shame for such a fine artist to have to sing on street corners, but Gary rather enjoys it (in spite of the guitar thefts, apparently)," Barry Kornfield observed in a March 1960 edition of *Sing Out!* magazine. "Once when singing in midtown Manhattan, a passer-by remarked he played very much like Rev. Gary Davis, to which Gary replied that he knew Reverend Davis quite well."

Davis met guitarist and teacher Stephan Grossman, who become one of his students, in 1960. Grossman encouraged Davis to release more blues and ragtime recordings, so on August 24, Davis went into the studios at Prestige/Bluesville Records. "Davis immediately became the focus of attention in the magnificent, cathedral-ceilinged studio," an observer said. "As the first notes of his fabulous guitar playing came through the speaker in the control room, it was evident this was to be Davis at his very best."

Now represented by Manny Greenhill of Folklore Productions, Davis played clubs and universities in Toronto, Los Angeles, Philadelphia, New York and Wisconsin. Royalties from a Peter, Paul and Mary version of one of his songs enabled him to buy a home. Bob Dylan became an admirer and included a version of one of his songs, "Baby Let Me Follow You," on his first album.

Davis appeared on British television in 1960, and toured the country with Muddy Waters and Brownie McGhee in 1964. He was back a second time in 1965, with dates in Birmingham,

Manchester, Liverpool, Bristol and London. "The man who took the most applause was the blind Negro guitar player and singer, the Rev. Gary Davis," the *Liverpool Echo* wrote after a June concert.

He toured England a third time in 1966. A year later, he performed on television in New York with Pete Seeger. From 1968 to 1970 he was a featured festival performer at Newport, Philadelphia and Harvard University. Annie was usually along when he appeared in the Northeast. Her appearances were always notable: "there is the added pleasure of hearing his wife at her seat, singing and humming throughout, as involved in the performance as Reverend Davis himself," a fan wrote. He made his first appearance on national TV in 1970, and during the same year, appeared in the documentary, "Black Roots," produced and directed by Lionel Rogosin.

In the early 1970s, Davis' career was still going strong. He toured England for the fourth time in 1971 and put in an appearance at the Cambridge Folk Festival. He went into the studio for Biograph in March of that year, wowing record officials with his (successful) insistence on recording songs in one take.

But England would be Davis' last tour and Biograph his last recording session. He played a concert at the Youth Development Center, Northport, Long Island, New York on April 24, and on May 5, suffered a fatal heart attack on his way to a concert in New Jersey. He was 76 years old. His funeral service was held at the Union Grove Church in New York. His widow, Annie, remained in New York after his death.

Davis was a preacher until the end and once stopped in the middle of a folk concert performance to start preaching to the crowd; he wouldn't stop the sermon until someone took him from the stage. As a performer, though, Davis was intense and usually satisfied his audiences. In black-and-white concert footage dating back to the heyday of folk music, Davis is performing "Children of Zion" on a bare stage, three white admirers at his side. About half-way through the performance, one of them is moved to pick up a banjo and join in. Davis barely bats an eye at his unexpected accompaniment; indeed, it appears to energize him; he yells out a few heartier "Amens" through the last chorus for good measure.

Sam "Lightnin'" Hopkins

I had the one thing you need to be a blues singer. I was born with the blues.

—Sam "Lightnin'" Hopkins

Lightnin' Hopkins' almost mythic life inspired a novel ("Mojo Hand," by Jane Phillips), and a documentary film, "The Blues According to Lightnin' Hopkins." It took him to England to perform for Queen Elizabeth and earned him considerable money he could never keep. He was a man with "no time for phonies" as one of his managers put it, and "a storm in his spirit," as more than one of his friends observed. He was alive when Sam Charters wrote his seminal book, *The Country Blues*, and occupies the last chapter of it, one that tries to capture both his flamboyance and his poetry.

Sam Hopkins was born in Texas some time around 1912. He was one of six children and lost his father while he was still a baby. His sister and four brothers were also musicians. Hopkins was encouraged by his mother to play the organ during church services. He built a guitar for himself when he was eight years old, cutting a hole in a cigar box, nailing on a plank for the guitar neck and stringing it with chicken wire. That same year, apparently, he and his family went to a meeting of the General Association of Baptist Churches at Buffalo, Texas. Sam and his family had driven up

49

from their Centreville farm for the event's Sunday afternoon picnic. The entertainer of the day was the great Blind Lemon Jefferson, whom Hopkins impulsively decided to accompany.

"I was so little and low they couldn't see me," Lightnin' recounted for Sam Charters. "He had a crowd of people around him and I was standing there looking at him play and I just went to playing on my guitar just what he was playing. So he say, 'Who's that playing that guitar?' So they say,'Oh, that's just some little boy knocking on the guitar.' He says, 'No he's just playing that guitar. Where he at? Come here, boy. And I went on over there where he was and he's feeling for me and I was so low he reached down and says, 'This here is what was picking that guitar?' They say, 'Yeah.' So he said, 'Do that again.' So I did, the little note again, the same one he had done. He said, 'Well that's my note. Boy you keep that up, you're gonna be a good guitar player.' So he went on and commenced to playing and I went on to playing with him. They put me on top of the truck and Blind Lemon was standing down by the truck. And me and him, we carried it on."

Lemon said to his uninvited accompanist, "Boy, you've got to learn to play it right." Hopkins said he always took those words to heart. Jefferson was one of the more important influences in his life. While still a youth he would see Lemon whenever the older man was down to play country suppers or in the town of Deep Ellum. Hopkins, in an interview, had nothing but praise for his mentor. "He was nice to me in every way," he said.

At the time Blind Lemon was a man with his share of problems. Born blind on a farm outside of Wortham, Texas in 1897, Lemon grew up an active though overweight child. His brother was killed by a train when he was 10. When he was 14, Lemon began to play the guitar and sing. He would go into Wortham for the day, sit in front of the feed or dry-goods stores and play for customers. By the time he was 20, Lemon was playing at picnics and parties and making plans to leave Wortham for Dallas. He found it tough to make a living in the city and for a time worked as a novelty wrestler in Dallas theaters to supplement his income. In the mid 1920s Lemon became an itinerant player, going as far east as Memphis, Tennessee, and Alabama. He recorded for Paramount and Okey Records in the 20s, but like most bluesmen never made much money at it. He came to a sad end in the streets of Chicago, dying a mysterious death out in the cold of a winter night. For such a man as Jefferson to take an interest in young Sam Hopkins says a lot about both of them.

When he was a teenager and beginning his years as a hobo Hopkins met another bluesman, the reclusive Skip James. Unlike Hopkins, Skip would not attain any kind of commercial success until the folk revival of the 1960s. Skip didn't like many people but he liked Hopkins. "Lightnin' kinda like myself," he'd say, approvingly. If Lightnin' felt the same way we'll never know, but when James later claimed to have given him guitar pointers, Hopkins would deny it: he and the older bluesman only gambled together, he said.

Hopkins had already begun playing with his other great musical influence, his cousin Alger "Texas" Alexander, during the 1920s. Alexander was an intermittently popular performer and one of the people Hopkins admired most. He "drove the first Cadillac I ever known to be," Lightnin' said. "Everybody admired him, you know, because colored people didn't have nothing. They didn't even have Model-T Fords then, and you know he come in a Cadillac."

During his early stints in Houston, Hopkins apparently used at least some of his free time for getting in trouble. He served time in Houston County Prison during the '30s for fighting. "I was kinda mean," was how he put it. He and his wife also hired themselves out to a farmer named Tom Moore, whose (apparent) dastardly deeds were forever immortalized in a song Hopkins wrote and named for him, though Lightnin' cannily changed the protagonist's first name to Tim. When he was in his 20s Hopkins was working a circuit between Dowling Street in Houston and West Dallas, with stops along the way at Crockett, Buffalo, Brenham and Palestine. He'd catch a ride in a friend's pickup when he was able or hop a freight train to get where he was going. He played at Texas farms with sizeable black work crews. By 1938, when he was 26 years old, Lightnin' was recording for the Gold Star label, which was based in Houston.

His first record for Gold Star, "Short-haired Woman," backed by "Big Mama Jump" sold between 40,000 and 50,000 copies, big numbers for what were termed "race records" in those days, sold primarily to a limited black audience. "Baby Please Don't Go," his second Gold Star release, sold 80,000. Hopkins decided that he was a star and was ready to act like one. Gold Star's Bill Quinn remembered Hopkins coming in on a Tuesday afternoon and asking for a $400 advance. Two days later, he was back for more. He had bought drinks for everyone in a local bar, he had explained, and the owner of the bar had given him an hour to come back with the money.

But Lightnin' had good reason to be optimistic. Twenty-two of Gold Star's master recordings were sent to Modern Records in L.A., giving Hopkins' records national distribution. His star on the rise, Hopkins recorded for Sittin' in With, Decca, Mercury, and Herald Records in the years between 1951 and 1954. Over the course of his career, Hopkins would record over 600 performances.

In 1959 Hopkins made his appearance in Charters' book and made a recording for the author the same year. In 1960 he toured the West Coast and appeared with Pete Seeger and Joan Baez at Carnegie Hall. He won the 1962 Downbeat International Jazz Critics Poll as New Star, Male Singer (after almost a lifetime of playing) and during one month in 1960, recorded 50 songs.

Blues and folk enthusiasts Chris Strachwitz and Mack McCormick were among those who saw Lightnin' play at Pop's Place in Houston. They had come to hunt up the protagonist of his song, Tom Moore.

"He was singing a slow blues," Strachwitz remembered. "And as he saw us come in the door, Lightning sang, 'Woah, this man come all the way from California just to hear poor Lightning play.' And from there (Lightnin') told us about the arthritis that was bothering him ... how his car barely made it to the tavern that night ... all of it was marvelously rhymed and made into a powerful blues performance."

"(The performance) was really like a conversation," Strachwitz concluded. "To me, he was the only real folk poet, the deepest bluesman I ever knew. His mind was just full of images."

Lightnin' appeared in the 1964 American Folk Blues Festival Tour in 1964; he was a sensation. Looking for quick cash, which he got, Hopkins released a ton of albums in the late 1960s-1970s.

Hopkins enjoyed both his fame and money. At last he followed in his cousin Alger's footsteps. "He always had a new Cadillac," said Billy Gibbons, guitarist for the Texas band ZZ Top. "Where he got the money nobody knows. He was a real flashy guy, dressed in the finest of fine. He had a constant cigar in his mouth with a little cigar holder."

"...I picked him up at the airport 1 o'clock in the afternoon for a gig," another musician, Robert Ross, said in an article published after Lightnin's death. "We rode around (for hours) looking for a hotel. He wanted to go to the expensive hotels ..."

But Lightnin' always said music was more than just income to him. He made this clear in the film made about him by Les Blank, Skip Gerson and Flower Films in 1969.

"When I play a guitar," he said in the film, *The Sun's Gonna Shine: The Blues According to Lightnin' Hopkins,* "I play it from my heart and soul ... The blues is something that the people can't get rid of. And if you ever have the blues, remember what I tell you. You're gonna hear this in your heart." Lightnin' carried a remarkably high opinion of himself and did so for most of his life, as witnesses could attest. "Lightnin' can't stand (imitation or comparison)," fellow bluesman Mance Lipscomb said. "He (thinks) he's the best (guitar player) in the world.

Joan Baez' manager booked Hopkins at Radcliffe University only to be shocked at seeing him descend from a Greyhound Bus clutching only a cheap and battered Stella guitar. "Don't worry," Hopkins told the man, who needn't have. As usual, Lightnin' put on a terrific performance.

Hopkins toured Europe as late as 1977, appearing at the Rotterdam Festival in the Netherlands. But bad health was catching up to him. An auto accident put him in a neck brace and restricted his tour schedule. His last professional gig was at Tramps in New York City in November, 1981.

Hopkins' naturally suspicious nature had caught up with him as well. He spent his last months and days a caustic and reclusive man, refusing to be photographed by photographers whom he knew would make money off his image.

"Lightnin' had no time for phonies," said Dr. Cecil Harold, a Houston surgeon who managed Hopkins during the last 12 years of his life. (Lightnin's nature also had a streak of self-pity; his favorite term for himself was "Po' Lightnin'.) Or maybe Skip James was right after all; he and Lightnin' were just kindred spirits. One observer said as much in the book, *Listen to the Blues*, noting that Hopkins "frequently plays concerts and universities ... and sometimes dismays his audiences by being (as) irascible, cantakerous and downright mean on stage as he is known to be off."

But in the end such speculations would hardly matter: Lightnin' was ill and growing weaker. In July of 1981, he underwent surgery for cancer of the esophagus. He died of pneumonia on January 30, 1982 in a Houston hospital and was lionized all over the country, in Texas newspapers and *Rolling Stone* magazine. A story goes that when some of Hopkins' friends filed past his casket they leaned close and noted an error. They said, "Yeah, they did a good job on ol' Lightnin', but where's his cigar?"

Like most interesting people, Lightnin' Hopkins was a dichotomy: he enjoyed the good life yet lived for his music. He performed constantly, recorded constantly, toured constantly and not strictly for the money. This inner compulsion may be explained by a conversation recorded in Les Blank's film:

"I got my education by sittin' around talkin' and lookin' at what this one do and what that one do," Lightnin' said. "You go to that field, there was your school with that hoe and plow that mule. Chop that cotton. Well, I said I wasn't going to do it. I didn't. I was just too tough. Why, I just know'd there was something in store for me, man. It wasn't nothin' on the end of that hoe handle for me. Chopping cotton, plowing that mule for six bits a day. That wasn't in store for me."

Mississippi John Hurt as he appeared in a
photo taken in 1964.

Mississippi John Hurt (1893-1966)

(Hurt) was like having our very own blues 'Yoda.'
—John Sebastian

In a public career that spanned only three years, "Mississippi" John Hurt won a slot on the "Tonight Show," gave a name to one of the best-loved bands of the '60s (The Lovin' Spoonful, after a phrase in one of his songs) and earned what was for a bluesman good money. He also made a lot of friends in three years. Seemingly everyone who met Hurt, except for perhaps Skip James, who married his step-niece and harbored a lasting jealousy of Hurt's career, loved him, praised him both publicly and privately, and mourned him when his life and career ended suddenly.

John Hurt was born in Teoc, Mississippi in 1893. He was one of 11 children (eight brothers and two sisters) and experienced the hard lot of the Southern black very early in his life. He quit school while only in the fourth grade and went to work for a farmer, Felix Healey, who lived across the way. He was playing guitar by the age of nine; his mother had bought it for him for the princely sum of $1.50. William Henry Kent, a close friend of Hurt's mother, was a guitar mentor for John. His was the first guitar Hurt ever played.

Hurt got his first taste of fame early in life, through a series of events that could only be described as serendipity. In 1928, when Hurt was in his 30s, scouts from Okeh Records came to a fiddle contest near his home. They heard fiddlers Willie Naramore (or Narmous) and William Smith play. When asked to recommend other likely prospects, both mentioned John Hurt. The scouts went to Hurt's house that same evening and got him out of bed. They listened as he played one song and offered him a contract before he finished a second. Hurt, with his extreme modesty, was reluctant to audition. "I told him, I can't sing very much less'n playin'," Hurt said. "Well I knew I couldn't sing o' way , but I sit over there and I worded it out and he says that's okay."

At a recording session in Memphis Hurt recorded "Frankie," which was issued that same year with "Nobody's Dirty Business" as a flip side. The record was an instant hit. In December he was invited to do another session for Okeh Records in New York City. He recorded "Stag O' Lee," "Candy Man," and other songs. His session resulted in seven more issued takes. But the Depression was creeping across the country and opportunities for rural bluesmen were few. John Hurt, along with countless other performers, went back into obscurity. Hurt would not record again for another 30 years.

Hurt went home to his wife, Jessie, and their son, John William. They and their small family (they had only one child) lived on a 200-acre farm owned by Reginald Ray Perkins. The property was also home to about 1,000 pigs.

Hurt supported his wife and son through farming and odd jobs. His only music-making was at family barbecues and picnics and at some radio stations in Grenada and Polk counties. Hurt's son, John William, remembered fondly how his father would play on the hill beside their home all night long. He even claimed that his father's syncopations and melodic style had come to him in a dream. He had simply awakened one day and started playing in this manner. Since the household had no record player, Hurt would have few strong musical influences other than himself. When critics later compared him to Blind Blake and Blind Boy Fuller, they'd be comparing him to musicians he had neither seen nor heard.

Hurt's life would have continued quietly and in a predictable fashion were it not for the folk revival of the 1950s and 60s. Young white blues enthusiasts were on the lookout for performers they only knew by name and a voice on old records. One of them, Tom Hoskins, went looking for Hurt via one of his records, a song called "Avalon Blues." He found Avalon, Mississippi, on an old map, and shortly thereafter, found Hurt. Hoskins recounted the journey in a memorial article written after Skip James' death: "I didn't have a very good car. I ran into this girl and she had a brand-new little Dodge Slant 6 and she really wanted to go to Mardi Gras. I said, 'I'd be happy to take you to Mardi Gras, and after that, I want to go up to Mississippi and see if I can find somebody."

Once he and his companion got to New Orleans, Hoskins phoned a friend back east and found out the bad news. The police had posted a 26-state bulletin for him: he was wanted for kidnapping, grand theft auto and violating the Mann Act. His companion, it seemed, was only 17 and the car belonged to her father.

"There wasn't much I could do about it then," he said. "If I got caught, I'd have to depend on her to explain that I was deceived." Fortunately, she did.

Since his many sources of income included bootlegging, Hurt mistook his visitor for a revenue agent — that Hoskins was from Washington, D.C. almost clinched the matter. But Hurt gave Hoskins a chance and watched, bemused, as recording equipment was set up in his living room and he was asked to play. By this time Hurt was not playing at all. He spent all his time tending the cattle on his landlord's farm (and boot-legging, one assumes). But Hurt obliged his visitor, and along with Jessie, reminisced for him. Hurt's playing had not diminished with age and in fact, to his white listeners, sounded better than ever.

Hoskins and some friends brought Hurt to what they knew to be a ready-made audience for him: the coffeehouse and folk circuit of the Northeast. Clarence Hood, a Meridian, Mississippi expatriate, owned the Ontario Place coffeehouse in Washington, D.C. He put Hurt onstage and the singer was an immediate hit. The young, long-haired, mostly white folk audience embraced the 60-something John Hurt, who responded in kind.

"John Hurt was the first blues musician ... with a very open attitude about sharing his guitar styles and licks," said John Sebastian, who often sat in and played harmonica at John's sessions. "Whereas other musicians would hold back their tracks, except in concert, John would happily take you into the dressing room ... and show you exactly what his hands were doing," Sebastian recalled.

Hurt started a trend: following his discovery, Sleepy John Estes turned up, as did Bukka White and Skip James. *Newsweek* and *Time* wrote about him; newsman Edward R. Murrow showed up to watch him play. His fans included comedian Bill Cosby and musician Tom Paxton. Sebastian named his band, The Lovin' Spoonful, after a phrase in Hurt's song, "Coffee Blues."

Hurt could play his old songs exactly the way they'd been recorded years ago, and his way of winning over audiences didn't hurt either.

"John had a lovely way of singing that almost made (his songs) like a child's lullaby," said Stephan Grossman, who knew Hurt and included a segment about him in his seminal 17-broadcast radio series on the blues.

Hurt found a home in Ontario Place, which happened to be a mid-Atlantic base for blues artists playing the coffeehouse circuit. One of those artists was Skip James, who married Hurt's step-niece, Lorenzo Meeks, after moving north.

James' handlers hoped he'd experience the same kind of popular success Hurt had enjoyed, but it was not to be. Skip's music was "too dense, too scary" for the coffeehouse crowd who embraced Hurt. Probably aware that he was forever being compared to his wife's uncle, Skip used every trick he knew to get back at Hurt. Backstage at Ontario Place he'd criticize Hurt's guitar technique and even offer him lessons. Claiming that Hurt crammed two many notes into his fingerpicking, James lectured him on "wasted motion." James lured Hurt into jam sessions and played complicated riffs and chord changes while Hurt gamely tried to keep up.

Hurt bore all of this with what one writer called "almost Christ-like acceptance." "Skip would play harder music to show that he was a better artist than John or to try to show John up," Lee Talbot, manager of Ontario Place, remembered. "Of course John would just have that gentle sort of smile and say, 'Boy, that Skippy sure can finger pick.'"

Hurt may have known people like Skip and realized they don't change. Or maybe he was having too much fun himself to be angry. Hurt got himself an agent, and his booking agency, based out of Cambridge, Massachusetts, named itself Avalon Productions in his honor.

He released "Folk Songs and the Blues" in 1963 and a live album and "Worried Blues" in 1964, all on the Piedmont label. He and his nemesis, James, both played at Newport.

But both men were only years away from dying. Skip suffered from cancer and died a lingering death in 1969. Hurt had preceded him, dying after a heart attack at Grenada Hospital on Nov. 2, 1966. He was 69. His posthumous releases include "Last Sessions" (Vanguard, 1966), "Avalon Blues" (Heritage, 1982), "Shake That Thing" (Blue Moon, 1986), and "Legend" (Rounder, 1997).

Stylistically John Hurt played outside the lines of what was thought to be Mississippi blues guitar. Those who heard him play say his syncopations and melodies were far closer to East Coast guitar styles than to the blues of Mississippi. Grossman probably puts it correctly when he calls Hurt more of a songster rather than a bluesman. Anyone who heard him play and sing the standard "You've Got to Walk That Lonesome Valley" can attest to that.

Nehemiah "Skip" James

I'd rather be the devil than be that woman's man...
>   —Skip James, "Devil Got My Woman"

I wouldn't hire him for a dance...
>   —Rev. Gary Davis, on Skip James

Nehemiah "Skip" James was as complex and contrary a bluesman as one might want. He was also a hard man to like, judging from the final days of his life. While he lay dying in a modest Philadelphia apartment, enduring pain which could not be eased by drugs, few friends came to comfort him.

Stephen Calt, James' friend and biographer and one of the few who came to see him at the end, said James' memories of blues glory were what sustained him through his suffering. James had been born in Mississippi in 1902, the only son of a cook and a bootlegger, and a man who came to music very early in his life. He was singing by the age of seven or eight and learning about guitar thanks to some local performers in Bentonia, his hometown. However, his most enduring memory of childhood was not of music, but of watching his father leave town. Wanted for questioning by federal revenue agents over his boot-legging activities, Edward James kissed his wife goodbye one night and disappeared into the woods. Skip was five years old at the time.

Skip grew up a solitary child, cared for by his grandparents whenever his mother, Phyllis, had to work for her employers at the Woodbine plantation.When Skip was 12 he and his mother reunited briefly with his father. They moved to Sidon where the elder James had been hiding out from the law. The reunion soured after father and son quarreled and Skip was beaten with a belt. Phyllis took Skip back to Bentonia in 1917 and eventually remarried. James attended the local high school, worked weekends at a sawmill, and took piano lessons from a cousin, Alma Williams.

Skip left high school to wander when he was 17. He joined a road construction camp near Ruleville, and cut logs for a sawmill in Yazoo County. On Saturdays, always, he was playing the blues. While on a job in Rankin County, Mississippi, Skip wrote his first song, "Illinois Blues."

He would find a musical mentor in Will Crabtree, a professional pianist, after moving to Weona, Arkansas in 1921. Crabtree, who played in one of the Weona juke houses, sometimes let the 19-year-old Skip sit in for him at the piano while he took his breaks. Crabtree was a major influence on both his piano style and his professional life: for the first time, James was playing for money. (He also began to enjoy less-savory pursuits in Weona — gambling and boot-legging.)

Skip came home to his mother in 1924 and settled into life on a plantation. He picked cotton during the day and played house frolics (a local term for parties) by night. He also appeared as a solitary singer on the streets. He soon picked up a partner and new mentor, Henry "Sport" Stuckey, whom Skip had first met as a child. Stuckey seems to have taught Skip the rare 'open E minor' guitar tuning (E-B-G-B-E), also known as cross-note, that he himself may have acquired from Bahamian soldiers while in France during World War I.

"We were just like two brothers," Skip said of Stuckey. The two of them would play back-to-back at parties, keeping a wary eye on the audience lest the more enthusiastic dancers get out of hand.

But whenever Skip went further afield, he'd do without Stuckey. Playing in Canton, Meridian, and Hattiesburg, Skip finally got to Jackson, the town where he may have acquired his nickname -- which at that time was Skippy, not Skip.

"I was never into anything too long or too deep," James would say later. "That's why I reckon they call me [Skippy]."

During the 1920s, Nehemiah "Skippy" James took it upon himself to become a top-flight blues pianist. (This is more remarkable than it sounds because most musicians of his day only really "played" one instrument; if they took up a second, they'd do little more than dabble in it.)

Skip met Mississippi's most famous blues pianist, Little Brother Montgomery, in 1927. "If you stay where you are," he warned Montgomery,

"I'm gonna catch up to you." All boasting aside, Skip allowed Montgomery's playing to have a subtle influence on him during this period. It was also during the late 1920s that Skip got married for the first time. He wed Oscella Robinson, the teenage daughter of a local clergyman, and took her to Dallas between 1928 and 1929.

Unfortunately, Oscella left Skip after becoming involved with a man who had been their traveling companion. James had already written and performed his signature tune, "Devil Got my Woman," by this point, but in the minds of those who knew him, and finally Skip himself, Oscella became "the Devil Woman." Her leaving was such a blow to Skip that he did not remarry for another 20 years.

In 1929, Skip took a protege, Johnnie Lee Temple, who became his assistant when he opened a music school in Jackson, Mississippi. Skip stayed away from the house frolic circuit during this period; when he performed it was as a solo street singer. One of Skip's contemporaries remarked that when he sang "Devil got my Woman" during a street performance he would sound so sorrowful that spectators paid him to stop.

In 1931, Skip auditioned for H.C. Speir, a Jackson Record dealer and a supplier of blues talent to record companies. Speir referred him to Paramount Records, which had coaxed hits out of Ma Rainey and Blind Lemon Jefferson. Guitar in hand, Skip boarded a segregated train to Milwaukee that winter and met Art Laibly, recording manager for Paramount. Laibly took him to Grafton and over the course of two days he recorded at least 18 songs. (Skip later insisted there had been 26.) His first record, "Hard Time Killin' Floor Blues," was released that spring.

Over the next year or so, Paramount released "22-20 Blues," "I'm So Glad" and "Special Rider". (These recordings may have also marked the first time he was called Skip. Paramount apparently thought "Skippy" would not do for a record label.) Skip was sure his records would make him rich and win him acclaim. Instead, he earned only $60 in royalties over his year with Paramount. Those records that did sell were mostly bought by black music fans, including the young Robert Johnson, who would do his own versions of "Devil" and "22-20". Already on hard times by the time it recorded Skip, Paramount finally succumbed to the Depression economy and went out of business in 1933.

Meanwhile, Skip's father had returned to Bentonia with a new wife and a new profession — he'd become a preacher. He requested a meeting with his son and implored Skip to leave the blues. Like most black Christians of his day, Edward James believed the blues was the devil's music. Skip initially resisted his father's entreaties, but finally agreed to go to Dallas and attend seminary school.

Skip's conversion shut down his musical career for 20 years. He even refused an attempt by

H.C. Speir to record him again in the '30s.

He spent three years in Plano, Texas, as his father's pianist. He worked as a piano tuner and repairman before joining the Dallas Jubilee Quartet, whose bookings were arranged by the deacon of the church. The group traveled to Tulsa, Oklahoma City, Kansas City and Wichita but disbanded after a year.

Meanwhile, Skip's protege Johnnie Temple had joined up with Charlie and Joe McCoy, who recorded "Devil Got my Woman" for Decca Records in 1934. Temple himself recorded "Devil" and "Cypress Grove" and later claimed to have written another Skip James standard, "Cherry Ball Blues."

When Edward moved to Birmingham, Ala., in 1935, Skip did not go with him. Instead he took up his former blues career in Bentonia for a while, until his father called him back to the fold. In 1937 he moved to Selma, Alabama, where Edward was the principal of a Baptist seminary. At the age of 40, Skip would be caught in a tug-of-war between both parents. In 1942 he was ordained as a Baptist minister, and the following year, as a Methodist minister, his mother's religion.

White jazz enthusiasts had begun to collect Skip James records in the 1940s, but it hardly mattered to their creator. He was by then working in a timber and steel camp where he would marry the camp cook, Mabel. A mine strike in 1948 sent Skip and his wife back to Bentonia, where he became a blues singer again. He may have been inspired by reports of Muddy Waters' success in Chicago, but he did not go there. He stayed in Bentonia, which still had a thriving "house frolic" circuit, and in Yazoo City with Henry Stuckey. Phyllis James died in February of 1950, and at the age of 48, Skip saw his father in Birmingham for the last time.

Blues continued to catch on in the 1950s, especially among young music fans. Guitarist Stefan Grossman would recall listening to a Skip James record over and over, trying to determine what guitar tuning he had used. (It was the cross-note, 'open E minor' tuning which came from the Bahamas by way of France and Henry Stuckey.) Musicologist Dick Spottswood heard "Hard Time Killing Floor Blues" for the first time in a music store and bought the record for $1.

The search was on for the source of these powerful songs. Gayle Wardlow, a Meridian, Mississippi native who regularly canvassed for blues records in the homes of elderly blacks, went looking for Skip James, unsure if he were alive or dead. In 1959, Sam Charters wrote *The Country Blues*, and compiled an album, "The Rural Blues," to go with it. The fragment of a James' song, "Little Cow and Calf," was featured on this record and a version of "Devil Got My Woman" appeared on "Really! the Country Blues" in 1961.

Skip was never too clear when recounting what he had been doing during the '50s and early '60s, although Johnnie Temple reported seeing him in West Memphis, Arkansas, in 1961. It is known that in Tunica, Arkansas, Skip sold fishing worms, drove a tractor and delivered fish and vegetables to New Orleans. In 1962, he left Tunica for Dubbs, Mississippi, and became a tenant on a plantation.

In 1964, budding guitarists John Fahey, Bill Barth and Henry Vestine (from the band *Canned Heat*) went went looking for Skip in Mississippi. They tracked him through his aunt, Martha Polk, and found him in a hospital bed recovering from surgery.

Skip was unimpressed with his discoverers, but when one of them offered him a guitar (he no longer owned one) he took it and began to work out a new song, appropriately called "Sick Bed Blues." A few days later, when he was discharged, his fans paid his medical bills and back rent and took him with them.

Sam Charters, in his book, *The Bluesmen*, described Skip's rediscovery: "He was still a little weak from the operation, and had done only a little playing; but he seemed ready to perform." Back at home, he played for the first time in seven years: "Devil Got My Woman," "All Night Long," and "Hard Time."

His new friends assured him that if he came back with them to Washington, D.C., he'd be as famous as Mississippi John Hurt. Skip needed little urging: he packed a suitcase, put on a dark suit and left Mississippi, never to return.

Another old bluesman, Son House, had just been rediscovered in Rochester, N.Y. On July 13, twelve days before the folk festival in Newport, Rhode Island, *Newsweek* covered both Skip and Son House in one story. "These two were the only great country blues singers still lost," the article rhapsodized. "No one knew if they were alive or dead. The search for these old-time bluesmen has always had a sense of urgency about it."

Skip greeted Newport with his own form of diffidence. When his future biographer, Stephen Calt, approached him at the festival and raved over his records, Skip said, "You like my records? I thought I sang like a girl." To another, would-be disciple, he said, "Why don't you take a bath?".

On July 25, at Newport, Skip performed four songs. "He sat expressionless as he waited to be introduced," Charters wrote. "But as he stepped slowly onto the small wooden platform ... he was trembling and nervous. After introducing him to three thousand people sitting under grey skies on the wet grass in front of the stage, it seemed as though he might not even be able to sing. His first notes as he began his guitar introductions were fumbled and incoherent: then his left foot suddenly began tapping, the guitar introduction emerged as the cross-note picking of 'Devil Got My Woman,' and his voice rose in the same clear falsetto... When he finished there was a long, excited roar of applause. ."

The following month, Skip set foot inside a recording studio for the first time in 33 years. He was booked at The Ontario Place, a Washington, D.C., coffeehouse, where John Hurt was a fixture. Skip, though, would not enjoy the same success.

John Hurt and Skip "were like the difference between tragic opera and some frivolous comedy," said Lee Talbot, who managed Ontario Place. "Everybody became quiet and thoughtful (when Skip played) — just the words of some of Skips songs send a shiver up your spine, and when he sang it, it was guaranteed to. (His music) made me think of some dark bayou with Spanish moss hanging off the trees, an eerie voodoo atmosphere. It made people feel uncomfortable ... but blues is supposed to make you feel uncomfortable."

Skip's attitude was a problem throughout this new phase of his career. "He was a true genius and he knew it," Dick Waterman, Skip's manager, once said. "He had a manner toward everyone that was aloof, condescending and patronizing." At other times Skip just refused to be nice. When blues enthusiast Dick Spottswood asked John Hurt whether he'd vote for Goldwater or Johnson in the 1964 election, Hurt replied that he wouldn't vote for either, since one or the other would be unhappy. When posed with the same question, Skip James said, "I'm voting for Skip."

Not everyone who knew Skip had sour feelings towards him. Skip lived with Spottswood while he was in Washington and became fast friends with Spottswood's wife, Louisa. "Skip was kind of an appealing rascal," she'd remember. "Very likable at times, very difficult at times — full of surprises."

James was by this time suffering from cancer. He underwent surgery in April of 1965 and, for a time, appeared to get better. He played piano in the Spottswoods' apartment, strolled around DuPont circle and fed the pigeons. He dropped his former handlers and began to record for Spottswood's company, to which he assigned the rights to his music. He recorded on July 28, 1965, and was paid $200. Skip James, Greatest of the Delta Blues Singers sold modestly but earned good reviews. (One critic would even compare Skip to Edgar Allen Poe and Vincent Van Gogh.)

Skip's marriage broke up about the same time he started feeling better. He left Mabel and moved to Philadelphia to be with his future wife, Lorenzo Meeks, an Avon lady who also happened to be John Hurt's step-niece. Their union lasted until his death, although it was hardly a roaring success.

"He gets up at night and sits and thinks," Lorenzo complained about her husband. "He won't tell anybody what's on his mind."

At the fourth annual Philadelphia Folk Festival, he connected with Dick Waterman, who'd set up a blues booking agency at 34 Parker Street in Cambridge.

His new album for Vanguard, "Skip James Today!" sold poorly, as did a release of "Devil Got My Woman," and "I'm So Glad." Skip grew ever more frustrated at his lack of royalties and low-paying concert gigs. Moreover, the coffeehouse circuit was drying up and the rock revolution was in full swing. Although rock did raise the profile of blues singers somewhat — blues was considered the precursor to the Beatles — this didn't translate into cash for Skip.

He did gain a windfall, though, from an unlikely source: a 21-year-old British rock guitarist named Eric Clapton. Clapton's group, Cream, recorded "I'm So Glad" for their Fresh Cream album in 1966. Clapton's version eventually netted Skip $6,000-$10,000. Two years later, Deep Purple recorded "I'm So Glad," and the cash came in again. Cavalier Magazine may have called Skip "the greatest blues singer of all time," but the financial rewards for his greatness were late and modest.

Skip played in Hamburg, Germany in 1967, but he was a sick man. The cancer continued to spread and by September, 1968, he was gravely ill. He was diagnosed inoperable at the University of Pennsylvania hospital, and sent home to die, which he finally did on October 3, 1969. Lorenzo was buried beside him eight years later. He left no other survivors.

Footage of a James' performance is included on Vestapol Productions' "Devil Got My Woman: Blues at Newport," shot by Alan Lomax Jr., at Newport in 1966. He is recorded playing three songs, including "Devil Got My Woman" and "I'm So Glad." James is three years away from dying, quite sick and not the guitar player he once was. Yet his chilling falsetto is intact and so is his diffident manner. In the moments before the final cut between songs, James is caught sitting silently on his chair, his face poker serious. He looks so uncomfortable during that moment you'd swear the camera was looking right into his soul.

BLIND WILLIE JOHNSON

This new and exclusive Columbia artist, Blind Willie Johnson, sings sacred selections in a way that you have never
heard before. Be sure to hear his first record and listen
close to that guitar accompaniment. Nothing like it anywhere else.

Record No. 14276-D, 10-Inch, 75c

I Know His Blood Can Make Me Whole
Jesus Make Up My Dying Bed

Ask Your Dealer for Latest Race Record Catalog

Columbia Phonograph Company, 1819 Broadway, New York City

Columbia
NEW PROCESS RECORDS
Made the New Way - Electrically
Viva-tonal Recording - The Records without Scratch

The only known likeness of Blind Willie Johnson,
used in this promotional material from Columbia
Records.

"Blind" Willie Johnson

Motherless children have a hard time ...
They haven't got nowhere to go.
Wandering around from door to door
Motherless children have a hard time
When mother is dead.
—Blind Willie Johnson,
"Motherless Children"

Because of his untimely death, "Blind" Willie Johnson missed the folk revival of the 1950s and 60s that made stars of many of his contemporaries. He never appeared at Newport and was not welcomed by adoring fans in Europe. He is a particularly elusive blues performer in that he left no thoughts of his own behind. There are no known interviews, no autobiographies; only his songs. He was photographed so seldom that only one image of him, that of a concert advertisement, still exists. He is one of the great, lost singers of his generation, though his music lives on. The young Eric Clapton was a fan and included a fabulous rendition of "Motherless Children" on one of his albums. The original version of a Johnson song, "Dark was the Night and Cold the Ground" was used in Pier Pasolini's film, "The Gospel According to St. Mark." Guitarist Ry Cooder later adapted the song as movie theme music for "Paris, Texas."

By the time blues historian Sam Charters came looking for Johnson in Beaumont, Texas, only Johnson's wife, Angeline, was left to tell his story. Johnson was born on a farm in Marlin, Texas, a small town east of the Brazos River, in 1898. Charters, who visited his birthplace, wrote that Marlin was a flat and colorless town, surrounded by narrow creeks, sandstone channels, brush, trees and plenty of dust. According to Charters, from the very beginning Johnson felt alone; perhaps it is easy to see why.

Willie was born a healthy boy with all his faculties. Willie's mother died when he was three or four years old. His father, George Johnson, remarried a few years later. When Willie was seven, his father caught his new wife with another man. He apparently gave her a beating of some sort. In return, she threw a pan of lye water in Willie's face. This act of vengeance cost the boy his sight.

What Willie Johnson thought of his stepmother and his disability is not known. But the loss of his eyesight certainly must have increased his sense of isolation — not to mention severely limiting his chances for any kind of success. A poor Negro boy in central Texas farm country had a hard enough time in life; a blind one had it even worse.

Perhaps it was not surprising, then, that Johnson turned to music and religion while he was still a boy. Charters wrote as how Willie would tell his father he was going to become a "beecher," his mispronounciation of the word "preacher."

Johnson was baptised into the Church of God in Christ early in life. He was also a familiar sight in the small downtown of Marlin. He sang gospel songs in the streets, taking tips in a tin cup pinned to his jacket.

By 1925, George Johnson had moved himself and his 27-year-old son to a farm outside of Hearn, Texas. (Hearn's claim to fame was its nine brickyards.) Johnson, who'd stood by his son through his disability, made sure the young man made it to town every morning to play. He would bring Willie to Hearn and leave him there while he went home to farm. Willie would sit under an awning and, just as he used to in Marlin, play for tips. His father would come to get him at the end of the day. Some Saturdays, Willie shared the streets with another blind street musician, the ubiquitous Blind Lemon Jefferson. Jefferson was yet another itinerant singer of his era — albeit a great one — who made his living off his wits and his voice.

Willie Johnson and Lemon Jefferson must have made a particularly striking pair in a town as quiet as Hearn. Lemon was stocky, plump and round-faced, while Willie was tall, thin, and gangling and had a thin moustache. Future blues great Mance Lipscomb, who lived in Brazos County, Texas, knew both men.

"I was a kid," Lipscomb wrote of Johnson in his book, *I Say Me For a Parable,* "In the teenage, maybe in nineteen-sixteen. He could sing all those verses, but he could play the guitar. He'd put it outa tune and I'd tune it up for him. And [the townspeople] give him a privilege to go to play, make his nickels on a Saturday, on the streets. Now if he wasn't a blind man, they wouldn't. They say, 'Well, yeah, you blind. You kin have the corner at Tex's Radio Place.' He had people from here to the highway, just [hundreds] a-people standin' right there on the streets. White and black, old colored folks and young ones an all."

As Mance remembered, Johnson asked the crowd if anyone there "could play a guitar. A lot of them people pick me out and say, 'Yeah, here's Mance Lipscomb. He kin play purdy good [guitar.]' [Johnson said], 'tell him come up here and tune up my guitar." From then on, [Mance] came every Saturday, "to tune it up. [Johnson] had a rough old guitar, rusty as a terrapin.

"Good songster," Lipscomb said of Johnson. "Loud voice." Johnson also taught Lipscomb a few songs, one of which he used to open a Berkeley Music Festival years later. It was "Motherless Children" and Mance would later describe how the song moved the audience to tears.

Johnson was a unique and unforgettable singer, considered brilliant by modern standards. He also played slide guitar in a style musicians agree was one of the best ever. He probably used a bottleneck, clasp-knife or metal ring to play slide. The technique of playing guitar with a knife was brought to the United States by Hawaiian troops that toured the country before World War

I. By the time he was in his mid-20s, his playing and singing had got him noticed. He signed on with Columbia Records and moved to Dallas. His first record was a hit, selling more than 15,000 copies. (Johnson usually sang religious songs and he did so at a time when they were quite popular.) Over the next three years Johnson recorded 30 songs for Columbia. Many of his tracks feature a woman singing back-up, and it was assumed for years the singer was his wife, Angeline. However, some evidence indicates that the backup singer may have been a former girlfriend, Willie B. Harris, who also belonged to the Church of God in Christ. Johnson did some tours with Blind Willie McTell, a street singer known for his high-pitched voice and big 12-string guitar. (For those who wonder how two blind men could travel together should remember the railroads, where the blind could ride for half-fare or not pay at all.) McTell was probably the antithesis of Johnson, recording almost anything for almost everyone (he used different names on different labels to avoid legal trouble) and taking his repertoire far beyond sacred songs. In 1940, McTell did some singing for John and Alan Lomax, then recording for the Library of Congress. Neither historian liked his style and did not release the records. McTell and Johnson must have made for an interesting pair, but their partnership was about to change. In 1927, Willie met and married Angeline.

Angeline told Charters that she heard a street singer singing the religious chant, "If I had My

Way" in the streets of Dallas one day. She walked along behind him and sang along, she said, until he noticed her. Angeline invited him to come to her home and sing hymns with her and he accepted. When she sang him her own version of "If I had My Way," Willie shouted. "Go on, gal, tear it up." After eating a dish of her seafood gumbo (she cracked the lobster claws for him), Willie asked her to marry him. She did, the very next day.

Willie was then 29 years old and about to do some of his best work on record. Columbia recorded him in Dallas the year he got married, and the selections included "Motherless Children," "If I had my Way (Samson and Delilah)," "Nobody's Fault but Mine," and "Dark was the Night and Cold the Ground," a wordless chant Willie had apparently borrowed from Baptist church services. (This practice was not unusual; many of the songs blues singers presented as their own were actually re-tooled folk songs they'd heard from someone else.)

His first record, "I Know His Blood Can Make Me Whole," was released in 1928. Willie had a powerful, and unforgettable, growl of a voice, and while listeners liked him some critics didn't know what to make of his style. Wrote one, "A few unusual singers should be mentioned ... Blind Willie Johnson's violent, tortured abysmal shouts and groans and his inspired guitar in a primitive and frightening Negro religious song, 'Nobody's

Fault But Mine' ...." (The critic, Abbe Niles, upon hearing "Motherless Children" threw up his hands and termed Johnson a brilliant guitarist and a religious fanatic.) Even Columbia's publicity department seemed unclear as to what Willie's music was about. An advertisement for "Motherless Children" reads in part, "A very popular artist sings a wonderful song of mother love. Everyone who loves mother will love this record."

After the Columbia sessions, Willie and Angeline moved on to Waco, then to Temple, and finally to Beaumont, where they bought a small house. Columbia approached him again in 1929 and brought him to New Orleans. He recorded on December 10 and 11, with a woman from one of the New Orleans churches singing soprano with him. He'd come to the sessions alone: Angeline had had to stay at home in Beaumont with their son, Willie Jr.

Willie stayed in New Orleans for nearly a month and a story has emerged that he was almost arrested, over a misunderstanding between him and the law. He was in front of the New Orleans Custom House, singing, "If I had my way." The song tells the story of Samson and Delilah and expresses Samson's wish to bring the pagan temple down and destroy his enemies. A policeman walked by as Willie was singing, thinking that the building Willie referred to was the Custom House, tried to arrest him. There's no record of how Willie got out of his brush with the law, but he did go home to Beaumont (stopping a few days in Lafayette, Louisiana, to see his father, who was making a new life for himself among a community of older Negro families) and eventually recorded about 30 songs in three and a half years with Columbia.

"I'm Gonna Run to the City of Refuge," with "Jesus Coming Soon" as a flipside was released in February, 1929. "I Just Can't Keep from Crying" and "Keep Your Lamp Trimmed and Burning" were released in June, to good notices. He and (presumably) Angeline recorded 10 songs together in a makeshift studio on College Avenue in Beaumont early the following year. Angeline sang solo on "If It Had Not Been for Jesus" and Willie was his usual stellar self. Years later, Charters singled out one of the 10, "You Gonna Need Somebody on Your Bond" as one of Willie's best. It was the last song Willie Johnson ever recorded.

Not even God sold well during the Depression. Record makers around the country were in serious financial trouble and the careers of singers like Willie were over, at least for the time being. He stayed in Beaumont with his wife and children, doing what he'd always done — street singing. He'd sing and play each day in downtown Beaumont along Forsythe Street. Johnson dressed neatly and conducted himself well on the job; the storekeepers of Beaumont remembered him as a gentle, dignified man. It was Angeline who'd lead him each day into the business district and they often sang together. They also sang at church benefits and Willie would accompany younger gospel singers, like the Silver Fleece Quartet.

A northern jazz revival in the '40s made Willie a household name in some circles, but he would neither know of it nor live long enough to enjoy it. In the winter of 1949, his house on Forest Street caught fire. The family got out safely; only a few furnishings and a guitar were lost. But the house, and everything in it, was soaked; Angeline had to spread newspapers over the bedding so they could go to sleep. Willie woke up sick the next morning but went out in the streets nonetheless to earn money for his family. It was a gallant but ill-advised gesture; singing for hours in the winter wind made his cold worse. He was dead of pneumonia within days. He was 51 years old. When Sam Charters came looking for him in the 1950s, Angeline would tell how, because of his blindness, the local hospital refused to take Willie in.

Johnson has been called "the most African of early blues singers." He was certainly that, but much more than it, too. He was more than a shouter, and more than a singer of gospel songs. His music could have a topical bent, particularly "God Moves On the Water," written after the sinking of the Titanic in 1912. The song tells of the ship's ill-fated launching, sinking and the frantic attempts of its passengers to cheat death. His songs take on a personal note even if he may not have intended for them to do so. One can hardly listen to "Motherless Children" without thinking of the young Willie, who lost his mother while he was still a boy.

He may indeed have been a lonely child—and a lonely man—but he had one constant companion: his guitar. It may be no wonder then that on numbers like "Dark was the Night and Cold the Ground" he and the guitar do seem to be having a conversation.

Mance Lipscomb

I never was a squabblin' man. I was a peaceful boy all a my whole life. [I] had my own mind made up ta be sociable an kind ta people.
—I ain't scared a nobody.
—Mance Lipscomb.

Mance Lipscomb displayed a unique sort of calm when he took the stage. He had never learned to read music, had little formal education, yet kept up such a commanding presence while he played that an onlooker might have sworn he had both. Unlike his counterparts Mance never got a chance to record until the folk revival hit, though he recorded plenty once given the opportunity. He was a professional bluesman in that he played for money every weekend, yet he rarely ventured more than 50 miles away from his home. Save for the two years he spent in Houston during the 1950s and the tours he did after white blues fans rediscovered him during the '60s, Mance Lipscomb spent his entire life in one place: Brazos County, Texas, where he was born.

The son of a fiddler and a woman who was half-black, half-Choctaw Indian, Mance was born April 9, 1895. His parents named him Bodyglin (or Beaux D. Glen, the French pronunciation), a name he understandably hated. As soon as he was old enough the boy renamed himself Mance and stayed Mance for the rest of his life. (How he came up with the name is not known.) His father, Charles, tried to introduce young Mance to the fiddle but the boy preferred the guitar. Being a practical sort, Charles Lipscomb taught his son to play chords and pick out bass runs so that Mance could back him up at Saturday Night dances. So young and short he had to perform atop a soapbox, Mance played along with Charles on reels, breakdowns, joke-songs and other tunes that pre-dated the Civil War. Mance pumped out a dance-style, bass beat that kept the time like a drum, setting the pace for his father's fiddle.

Mance had a world of praise for his father as a musician. "He could make that [fiddle] talk, man," Mance said. "He could make it say, "Our Father Who Art in Heaven." One thing Charles Lipscomb could not, or would not, give his son was time; he left Mance's mother when the boy was 12 years old.

Mother Janie Lipscomb was the one to buy Mance his first real guitar. A gambler who strolled through their cotton fields offered it to her for a dollar and a half, or in those days, three days' wages. Janie took him up on the offer, probably because she understood her son's need to make music as much as his father did.

"Mama had a good strong voice," Mance would tell his biographer, Glen Allyn. "[But] she never would sing wit' Papa. Papa an' her lived disagreeable."

"[She] was a one-man woman, [Father was] a twenty-woman man."

A song called "Sugar Babe" was the first he

learned to play. "Reason I know it so good," Mance said later, "[was because] I got a whippin' about it. Come out of the cotton patch to get some water and I was up at the house, playin' the [guitar] and my mother come in; whopped me 'cause I didn't come back [to the cotton patch like she told him to]."

A boy who has to work as hard as Mance did never makes it far in school, and Mance didn't. He quit in the third grade after his older brother, Charlie, had left home to seek his fortune. There was plenty at home to keep Mance busy, even beyond all the work and his guitar-playing. Mance's 10 brothers and sisters all played instruments; Charles Jr. and Ralph played guitar, Annie was on vocals. When circus carnival musicians Richard Dean and Hamp Walker came to town Mance got to hear their versions of vaudeville and minstrel show songs. The crank-up Victrola one of his neighbors probably owned played Bessie Smith, Memphis Minnie and Big Bill Broonzy. Mance even got some last minute schooling from a neighbor, George Jones. Jones tutored Mance when he was in his teens and Mance gave him credit for the elegant penmanship he carried with him into adulthood and old age.

Mance was unique among bluesmen in that (despite his being a homebody) his path seemed to effortlessly cross with those of the other bluesmen of his era. He also seemed to like his colleagues (another rarity) and easily talked about them with his co-author Alyn. His reminiscences are an important part of the historical record of that era. In the fall of 1917, Lipscomb went to Dallas to pick cotton and heard about a musician who played under a live oak tree on the Houston & Texas Central tracks, down under the Deep Ellum street. This was Blind Lemon Jefferson, from Wortham, Texas. Mance went to see, and hear, him.

"He's standin' there on the ground, on the railroad tracks playin' [East St. Louis Blues]," he said. "They give him permission ta play in a certain district in Dallas. Right off the railroad track: that was his gatherin' ground ... I don't know how much money he made, but he made his livin' that way. He was a big stout fella, played dance songs, never a church song." Jefferson wasn't always welcome in Dallas, or indeed anywhere, Mance remembered. The authorities would "[forbid] him right out of town," he said. "But the law would let Lemon [play outside the city limits]. He's a big loud songster and he'd have all that gang a people gatherin' round 'im."

Jefferson's audience would move out of the town with him, to the place where he'd been banished.

In central Texas, Mance met another blind singer, Willie Johnson, a slide guitarist who used metal pipes or glass bottlenecks to create his sounds. (Lipscomb was wont to tune Johnson's guitar for him whenever he and Johnson were in the same town.) Johnson taught him at least two songs, "Motherless Children" and "God Moves on Water."

Mance knew of Huddie "Leadbelly" Ledbetter —then serving time in the Sugar Land penitentiary near Houston. Ledbetter went on to fame, notoriety (and more prison time) but he and Mance never met. "Never did see him," Mance said. ""I didn't wanta meet them convicts."

He met the singer Lightnin' Hopkins in 1938, when Hopkins was playing in Galveston. Lightnin' had already made a name for himself in Texas, wore nice clothes, made decent money. Mance liked him, though he and the flashy Lightnin' couldn't have been more different.

"In Houston, he got a big name," he said. "'Cause he was a good songster. [He] is an E [chord] man. He's a great friend of mine. That rascal kin sing. Nobody in the world ever played none a Lightnin' Hopkins' songs [like he could]. Never will play it. 'Cause he got his own way playin' it."

In the 1920s, Mance's own playing caught the attention of singer Jimmie Rodgers, who asked Mance to tour with him. Mance said no and never regretted it. "Jimmie Rodgers come through right down there in my town" in 1922, he said. "They wanted me to go off with him ... but it [wasn't] none a my time to go." Mance was probably thinking of his family obligations when saying no to Rodgers. He and his wife, Elnora, were supporting their relatives and their mothers. Altogether through their long marriage they would support sixteen family members. Mance Jr., their only child—definitely not his father's son—presented them with four (ex) daughters-in-law, twenty-six grandchildren (some of whom they adopted) and thirty great-grandchildren. This extended family came in handy in one way; many hands made it easier to harvest the cotton each year.

Mance worked for a man named Walter Mobley through the 1930s and '40s in that inequitable system known as sharecropping. Mance described the arrangement as "one bale to him, one bale to me," and he'd usually be the one to lose money. Mance apparently turned a profit (as little as $150 once, as much as $700) only two or three seasons. "I have worked in Houston, in the brickyard, lumberyard, farmed mostly all my life," Mance said. "I've done a lot of different things in my life, but I never worked as hard as I did on the farm."

The 1930s and 40s were also the era of the juke joints, like the Big Wheel and Nolan's place around where Mance lived. Radio had come into the neighborhood and tunes like "Key to the Highway," by "Big Bill" Broonzy were the pop hits. Mance went to work for a man named Johnny Sommers after World War II, moving his family and mules to the Bluffs of Washington County. For the first time, Mance stopped plowing with mules and used a tractor. In 1950, Mance's tenant house burned to the ground and and the fire took everything with it, including Mance's guitar and Elnora's false teeth. (They managed to save a pair of overalls on the clothesline and their night clothes.) Figuring it was as good a time as any to make a fresh start, Mance moved them to Houston. He played guitar in a Houston beer joint for $10 a night and worked a day job in a lumber yard for $58 a week. A freak accident at the lumberyard fractured his neck (a load of timber fell on him) and an equally freakish encounter with a personal injury lawyer on the street eventually won him a $3,500 settlement from his employer. (Mance had to borrow money for rent while he waited for the settlement money.) Mance and Elnora moved back to Novasota and bought two and a half acres from Mance's Uncle Jim and Mary Oliver. They built a house out of salvaged lumber and settled in. It was the first home they'd ever owned.

In 1960, folklorist Mack McCormick and Chris Strachwitz, an entrepreneur and music enthusiast, were traveling through Texas on a quixotic mission. Strachwitz and McCormick had decided to hunt down Tom Moore, the evil protagonist of a Lightnin' Hopkins song. (Though why, since the song vilified him, Moore would even want to be found is another question). While passing through Brazos County they asked the locals if there were any good guitar pickers around. The locals sent him to Mance. They arrived on Mance's porch after he had spent the day cutting grass along the highway. Mance thought the two young white men were policemen (although he had nothing to fear; unlike his contemporaries he doesn't appear to have been a bootlegger) but they soon convinced him otherwise. That evening they recorded over two albums of material in Mance's living room. They needed only one take per song even though Mance was playing an acoustic Harmony guitar he'd never seen before. Strachwitz signed Mance to Arhoolie Records, the record label which he'd founded. Mance's first album was issued in 1961. He got an invite to the Berkeley Folk Music Festival that same year and had his first look at the Golden Gate bridge. He appeared on the same concert bill as Pete Seeger, Jean Ritchie, Sam Hinton and others. He was paid $300 for his appearance and played before 41,000 people. He started out his set with "Motherless Children," taught to him by Johnson. Midway through the song that day he was tactfully told by a festival employee that his selection was depressing the audience and could he please play something else.

Nonetheless, Mance was a hit. In 1962, he performed at the Houston Hootenanny. He was at Newport in 1965 and made appearances in Ann Arbor, Monterey, Los Angeles and Miami. He took part in the 1968 and 1970 Smithsonian Folklife Festivals and the 1973 Arkansas Bluegrass festival. The man who'd never been out of Texas mingled easily with Bob Dylan, Joan Baez, Sonny Terry and Brownie McGhee and got good at flirting with airline stewardesses. ("A rascal," Mance said of Dylan. "A good friend of mine. He got too much money offa one a my songs an he won't say nothin' about it.") One of his new friends, John Lomax Jr., financed the Les Blank/Skip Gerson documentary of Mance's life and career, "A Well-Spent Life," in 1970.

Mance also encountered Shirley Dimmick, a white blues singer and the first woman to travel with an all white band. She had been tipped off by someone in New York to go hear Mance in Texas; she did and was impressed. He played in an impromptu string and bass band, composed of his guitar, a piano, harmonica and gutbucket (or washtub), at a Houston country juke joint that night. At the time, Dimmick was giving a longhaired, raspy-voiced white girl voice and blues lessons. Dimmick took care to get her pupil together with Mance Lipscomb. The student's name was Janis Joplin. (Mance probably liked her, just as he liked everyone). Taj Mahal was another of Mance's former students. Mahal played the world over using piano, guitar and vocals and mixing blues, jazz and Caribbean styles.

Over the years, Mance performed with Seeger, the Grateful Dead, Arlo Guthrie, Junior Wells, Howlin' Wolf, and Willie Nelson. At age seventy-seven, Mance had lost none of his energy: he could still play 17 hours out of a day. He was also making up for lost time. He recorded seven albums for Arhoolie, and three for Reprise. He enjoyed both his fame and his famous fans; former president Lyndon Baines Johnson was among them. LBJ, wife Lady Bird and daughter Lynda Bird came to the Kerrville Folk Festival expressly to see Mance play. Mance even went on a

Gambian postage stamp (never an American one) and put his footprints in front of Grauman's Chinese Theater in Hollywood. Mance seems to have taken it all with the affability that was his trademark.

In 1973 author Glen Alyn came to Novasota hoping to write Mance's biography. He found Mance and Elnora living much as they always had, despite Mance's fame: simply and sparely. (This may not have been entirely by choice; like most blues musicians Mance simply didn't get rich.) Alyn recorded extensive tapes of Mance singing and playing and telling the story of his life and what he knew of his fellow blues musicians. (These tapes are in the permanent collection at the University of Texas in Austin.) The result, "I Say Me For a Parable," is a nearly word-for-word transcription of Mance's thoughts coupled with Alyn's research into his life. Alyn did his best to preserve the flavor of Mance's speech and idioms. The tapes are also available for listening in Austin.

Alyn came away impressed with Mance's gentlemanly air on and off the stage, his lack of bitterness at the curves life had thrown him and his resolute kindness to his fellow human beings. One of the hallmarks of Mance's relationships was that he never seemed to mind dealing with people who were different than himself.

"I never was a squabblin' man," Mance told Alyn. "I was a peaceful boy all a my whole life. [I] had my own mind made up to be sociable an kind to people." On July 24, 1974, Mance suffered a stroke and fell ill with pneumonia. Taj Mahal, who would write the foreword to Mance's autobiography, came to the World Headquarters of Armadillo Records to play a benefit for his mentor. The concert raised $3,000, enough to pay the rest of Mance's medical bills. Mance Lipscomb died on January 30, 1976. He was 80 years old. He and Elnora had been married for sixty-two years. He had had an active recording and national performing career for only fifteen.

Bibliography

Bruynoghe, Yannick. *Big Bill Blues*. William Broonzy's Story as told to Yannick Bruynoghe. Da Capo Press, N.Y., 1955.

Calt, Stephen. *I'd Rather Be the Devil; Skip James and the Blues*, Da Capo Press, New York, 1994.

Charters, Samuel B., *The Bluesmakers*. Da Capo Press, New York: 1967

Charters, Samuel B. *The Bluesmen,* Oak Publications. New York: 1967.

Charters, Samuel B., *The Country Blues,* Da Capo Press. New York: 1959.

Collins, John. *The Blues*. Salamander Books. London, England: 1997.

Davis, Francis. *History of the Blues*. Hyperion, New York: 1995.

Dunaway, David King. *How Can I Keep from Singing: Pete Seeger*. McGraw-Hill, New York. 1981.

Lipscomb, Mance. *I Say Me for a Parable: The Oral Autobiography of Mance Lipscomb, Texas Bluesman.* As told to and Compiled by Glen Alyn, W.W. Norton & Co., New York. 1993,

Oliver, Paul. *Conversations with the Blues*. Cambridge University Press. Cambridge, England: 1965.

Tick, Judith. *Ruth Crawford Seeger: A Composer's Search for American Music*. Oxford University Press: 1997.

Tilling, Robert. *Oh, What a Beautiful City: a Tribute to Gary Davis*. Paul Mills Press, Jersey, England: 1992.

Courtesy of Rashidah Z. Hakeem, assistant blues archivist/music librarian, Blues Archive, The University of Mississippi, University, Miss. 38677:

Alvarez, Rafael. "Lightnin' will strike the blues no more," The Baltimore Sun, Tuesday, Feb. 2, 1982.

"Classic Blues Albums, Skip James - Today!" Page 18-19. Blueprint. March, 1993.

Dean, Eddy. "Skip James' Hard Time Killing Floor Blues," Washington City Paper, Vol. 14, No. 25-Dec. 1. Pages 24-32.

Demmerle, Linda. "Cotton Picking," January/February 1995. Acoustic Guitar, Pages 121-126.

Grossman, Stefan. (Interview by Tom Hoskins) "Scrappin' the heart and Knockin' them back," A classic interview with the legendary Mississippi John Hurt. Sing Out! Vol. 39 #4, March/April 1993.

Jones, Max. "Skip James," The Blues Page, Melody Maker, Oct. 18, 1969, Page 18.

"Lightnin' Hopkins, Biography," Verve, a division of Polygram, Worldwide Plaza, 325 Eighth Avenue, New York, NY 10019.

"Little John," Time, September 27, 1963, Page 64.

Loder, Kurt. "Lightnin' Hopkins: 1912-1982," Rolling Stone, March 18, 1982, Pages 17-18.

Moore, Bob. "Lightnin' Hopkins - Lightnin'" Concert-News, Issue 57, Vol. 5, No. 14, August 20-31, 1977.

Seeger, Mike. "Elizabeth Cotton - Folk Music Legend," Sing Out, Page 48-49. Aug. 1, 1987.

Sokolow, Fred. "Lightning Strikes," September/October 1994. Acoustic Guitar. Page 84, 90-91.

Disc and Videography

Country Blues Guitar/A Series of 17 Radio Broadcasts, Vestapol Productions/a division of Stefan Grossman's Guitar Workshop.

Devil Got My Woman, Blues at Newport (From the Alan Lomax Collection), featuring Howlin' Wolf, Skip James, Son House, Bukka White and Rev. Pearly Brown. Notes by Mark Humphrey. Vestapol Productions/a division of Stefan Grossman's Guitar Workshop.

Elizabeth Cotten. Notes by Mark Humphrey. Rounder Records, One Camp Street, Cambridge, MA 02140 1994, Vestapol Productions/a division of Stefan Grossman's Guitar Workshop Inc.

John Fahey/Elizabeth Cotten, Rare Interviews & Performances from 1969, Notes by Mark Humphrey. Rounder Records, One Camp Street, Cambridge, MA 02140 1994, Vestapol Productions/a division of Stefan Grossman's Guitar Workshop Inc.

Legends of Country Blues Guitar, Vol. 1, featuring Big Bill Broonzy, Mississippi John Hurt, Son House, Mance Lipscomb, Rev. Gary Davis, Robert Pete Williams, Josh

White and Brownie McGhee. Vestapol Productions/a division of Stefan Grossman's Guitar Workshop.

Legends of the Blues, c. 1990, CBS Records, 606 Fifth Ave., New York, NY 10101. Notes by Paul Oliver.

Lightnin' Hopkins, Rare Performances 1960-1979. Vestapol Productions/a division of Stefan Grossman's Guitar Workshop. Notes by Mark Humphrey.

News & The Blues: Telling it Like It Is. 1990 CBS Record, 606 Fifth Ave., New York, NY 10101. Notes by Pete Welding.

Index